SAY IT LOUD, AND SAY IT PROUD

Kvelling, It's Part of Our DNA

ISBN-13: 978-1981637317
ISBN-10: 1981637311

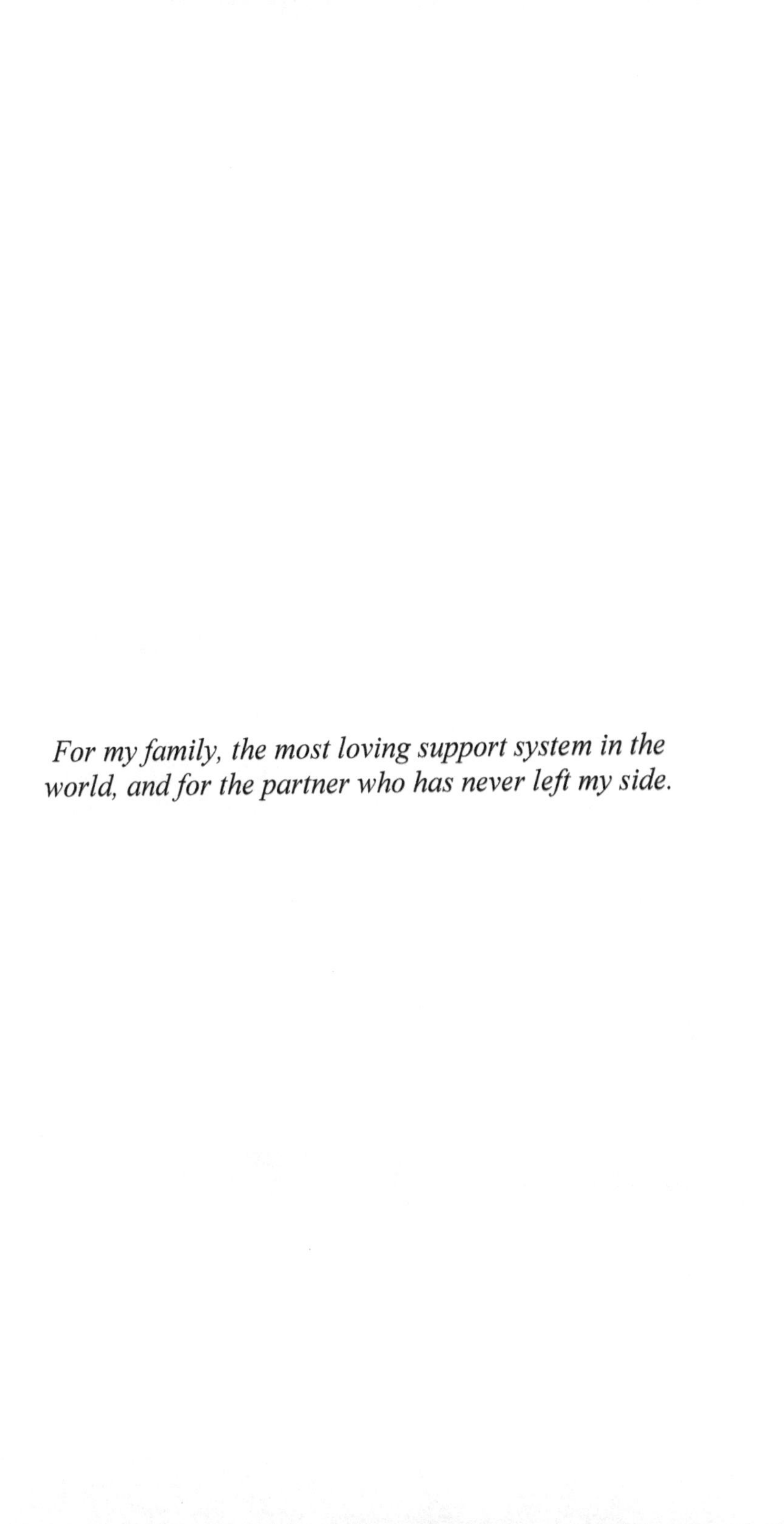

For my family, the most loving support system in the world, and for the partner who has never left my side.

PROLOGUE

"I will insist the Hebrews have [contributed] more to civilize men than any other nation. If I was an atheist and believed in blind eternal fate, I should still believe that fate had ordained the Jews to be the most essential instrument for civilizing the nations. They are the most glorious nation that ever inhabited this Earth. The Romans and their empire were but a bubble in comparison to the Jews. They have given religion to three-quarters of the globe and have influenced the affairs of mankind more and more happily than any other nation, ancient or modern."

John Adams, Second President of the United States, from a letter to F.A. Van der Kemp (Feb. 16, 1808), Pennsylvania Historical Society

Index

- Goliath was a 40 point favorite over David.
- Believe. Achieve. Succeed.
- Everyone was needed to build America, not just the "right people."
- The grand prize was life.
- The challenges of statehood.
- Sometimes, even to live, is an act of courage.
- "Jesus was a Jew, yes, but only on his mother's side."
- Everybody enjoys kvelling
- And then there's Chutzpah
- Torah…Torah…Torah...
- About this idea of being the "chosen people."
- Imitation is the sincerest form of flattery.
- A Testament of Hope
- "Education is not the filling of a bucket, but the lighting of a fire."
- Rewind
- The voices of a people…
- "The Blame Game…"
- The future is always beginning today.

INTRODUCTION

The dictionary defines the word "kvell" as to feel proud to the point of tears; to be extraordinarily pleased; to be bursting with pride. I define the word "kvell" as...

Moses, Abraham, Maimonides, Solomon, Levi Strauss, Richard Rodgers, Oscar Hammerstein, Albert Schweitzer, Harry Houdini, Samuel Goldwyn, Simon Wiesenthal, Marc Chagall, Nathan Rothschild, Mae West, Billy Wilder, Franz Kafka, Lillian Hellman, J.Robert Oppenheimer, Edwin Land, George Burns, Al Jolson, Anne Frank, Jonas Salk, George Gershwin, Golda Meir, David Ben Gurion, Marcel Proust, Man Ray, Jack Benny, Carl Sagan, Gypsy Rose Lee, William Paley, Edna Ferber, Louis Brandeis, Sigmund Freud, Elie Wiesel, George S. Kaufman, Adolph Zukor, Irving Berlin, David Sarnoff, Alfred Dreyfuss, Leonard Bernstein, Arthur Miller, Max Fleischer, Jerome Robbins, the Three Stooges (Larry, Moe, and Curly), Jesse Lasky, Jesus of Nazareth, Albert Einstein, Saul Bellow, Erica Jong, Sam Spiegel, Aaron Spelling, Fannie Brice, Baruch Spinozo, Sholom Aleichem, Henry Kissinger, Benjamin Cardozo, Bernard Baruch, J.D. Salinger, Bernard Malamud, Mel Allen, the Marx Brothers (Groucho, Harpo, Chico, Gummo, and Zeppo), Rod Serling, Benny Goodman, Eddie Cantor, Danny Kaye, Jack Warner, Milton Berle,

David Belasco, Howard Cosell, Moss Hart, Paddy Chayefsky, Red Buttons, Aaron Copeland, Solomon R. Guggenheim, Harold Arlen, Mel Blanc, Samuel Irving Newhouse, Moses Annenberg, Joseph Pulitzer, Studs Terkel, Walter Winchell, Louella Parsons, Rube Goldberg, Rabbi Meir Kahane, S.J. Perelman, Superman, Sandy Koufax, Woody Allen, Bob Dylan, Mel Brooks, Jerry Lewis, Lawrence Tisch, Sumner Redstone, Itzhak Perlman, Ruth Bader Ginsburg, Barbara Walters, Adam Sandler, Kirk Douglas, Barbra Streisand, Billy Crystal, Nora Ephron, Neil Diamond, Arthur Goldberg, Paul Simon, Neil Simon, Jerry Seinfeld, Dianne Feinstein, Isaac Stern, Bette Midler, Stephen Sondheim, Larry King, Barry Manilow, Leonard Nimoy, Stephen Spielberg, Fran Drescher, Barbara Boxer, Burt Bacharach, Ann Landers, Ruth Westheimer, Annie Liebowitz, Judy Sheindlin, Pauline Kael, William Safire, David Halberstam, Ariel Durant, Mitch Albom, Alfred Eisenstadt, Alfred Stieglitz, Margaret Bourke-White, Shel Silverstein, Fred Hirschhorn, Marcus Loew, Stephen Wise, Red Auerbach, Larry Gelbart, John Frankenheimer, Richard Avedon, Fred Friendly, Mark Goodson/Bill Todman, Norman Lear, Shari Lewis, Benjamin Netanyahu, Lorne Michaels, David Susskind, Brandon Tartikoff, David Wolper, Emma Lazarus, Jason Alexander, Ed Asner, Roseanne Barr, Sid Caesar, Elliot Gould, Al Franken, Alan King, Hal Linden, Jackie Mason, Debra Messing, Bess Myerson, Jerry Ohrbach, Sara Jessica Parker, Gilda Radner, Tony Randall, Carl Reiner, Rob Reiner, Michael Douglas, Geraldo Rivera, Henry Winkler, Mike Wallace, Howard Stern, Jerry Springer, Leslie Stahl, Mort Sahl, Lewis Rukeyser, Joan Rivers, William Shatner, Michael Eisner, Art Buchwald, Al Capp, Max Shulman, Donna

Karan, Ralph Lauren,   Estee Lauder, Alan Greenspan, Joseph Lieberman, Michael Dell, Sergey Brin, Wolf Blitzer, Mark Spitz, Marlee Matlin, Ben Stiller, Dustin Hoffman, Theodore Bikel, Carrie Fisher, Jerry Stiller, Natalie Portman, Howie Mandel, Maury Povich, George Axelrod, Paul Newman, Clifford Odets, Dorothy Parker, Roberta Peters, Chaim Potok, Steve Jobs, Rodney Dangerfield, Sammy Davis, Jr., Lenny Bruce, Isaac Asimov, John Steinbeck, Abigail Van Buren, the Ritz Brothers, Marcel Proust, Harold Pinter, Calvin Klein, Artie Shaw, Moira Shearer, Beverly Sills, Totie Fields, Arthur Fiedler, Betty Friedan, Alan Jay Lerner, Fritz Loewe, Fritz Lang, Alan Alda, Herb Alpert, Kitty Carlisle, Goldie Hawn, Vladimir Horowitz, Yasha Heifetz, George Jessel, Victor Borge, Henny Youngman, Ernst Lubitsch, Marcel Marceau, Marilyn Monroe, Isaac Mizrahi, Flo Ziegfeld, Leo Rosten, Gustav Mahler, Felix Mendelssohn, Ethel Merman, Norma Shearer, Boris Pasternak, David Copperfield, Ethan & Joel Coen, Jeffrey Katzenberg, David Geffen, Ted Koppel, Sheldon Adelson, Steve Wynn, Carl Icahn, Ronald O. Perelman, Ronald Lauder, Leonard Lauder, Edgar M. Bronfman, Jr., Henry Kravis, Lauren Bacall, Tony Curtis, the flags of Israel and the United States, Theodore Herzl, Solomon Schechter, Arthur Murray, Elizabeth Taylor, Nathan Sharansky, Bella Abzug, Peter Lorre, David Selznick, Jacob Javits, Aaron Sorkin, Carl Laemmle, Abraham Ribicoff, Ed Wynn, Sophie Tucker, Edward G. Robinson, Paul Muni, Gertrude Berg, Judy Holliday, Bob Dylan, Jules Styne, Michael Kidd, George Cukor, Norman Lear, Arthur Penn, Arlen Specter, Ben Hecht, Lawrence Kasdan, David Merrick, Harold Prince, Moses Montefiore, Jerry Bruckheimer, Stanley Kubrick, Henry

Morgenthau, Sr., Haym Solomon, Billy Rose, Herbert Lehman, Dinah Shore, Zero Mostel, Hedy Lamarr, John Garfield, Mel Torme, Jamie Lee Curtis, Hank Azaria, Buddy Hackett, Michael Landon, Richard Dreyfuss, Barney Frank, Charles Schumer, Stanley Donen, Mervyn LeRoy, Connie Chung, Samuel Z. Arkoff, Theda Bara, Baron Edmund Rothschild, Louis B. Mayer, and Benjamin Disraeli. And, dear readers, that's just for openers.

I know it's not polite to brag, but why the hell shouldn't we be proud? And yes, I did say Superman.

THE INCREDIBLE POWER OF 2 CENTS

Go to your local bank and exchange a $10.00 bill for 1000 pennies. Spread the pennies on your kitchen table (or your bed, or the floor). The 1000 pennies represents the world's population (1000 pennies = 7.5 billion people). Now take two of those pennies and put them in your hand. You are now holding the world's entire Jewish population. Two out of a thousand. Doesn't seem like much, does it? Over 7.5 billion people on the planet. Maybe 14 million Jews. That's less than .002 of 1% of the world's population. You want to know why the word "kvell" is part of our DNA? It's because of those two pennies.

Winston Churchill, Prime Minister of England, put it this way: *"Some people like the Jews and some do not. But no thoughtful man can deny the fact that they are, beyond any question, the most formidable and the most remarkable race which has appeared in the world."*

He was, and still is, right. We definitely don't win many popularity contests on our home planet. My guess, we never will. Our numbers are incredibly small. And yet, what we have achieved is staggering. Our contributions, monumental. Our gifts, eternal.

We Jews have done things which are beyond the imaginable. Our forefather, Abraham, introduced the world to high ethical standards and the belief in Heaven. We brought the world the Ten Commandments. We violated the rules of history by staying alive, totally at odds with common sense and historical evidence. We outlived all our former enemies, including vast empires such as the Romans and the Greeks. We angered the world with our return to our homeland after 2000 years of exile and after the murder of six million of our brothers and sisters.

We built, in the wink of an eye, a democratic State which others were not able to create in even hundreds of years. We built living monuments, such as the duty to be holy, and the privilege to serve one's fellow man.

We introduced the world to one God.

Much of Western civilization is framed in terms of concepts first articulated by the Jews. We have a higher purpose of life and the need to be honorable.

We've had our hands in every human progressive endeavor, whether in science, medicine, psychology or any other discipline, while totally out of proportion to our actual numbers. We gave the world the Bible, and even their Savior.

We were the first people to believe in a single God. Monotheism is perhaps the single greatest gift to all mankind. For the Jewish people, God is depicted as the one who created the world and guides its history. And from this uncomplicated belief was born the Old Testament.

Today, Christianity and Islam account for more than half the world's 7.5 billion people, but they both began with Judaism.

Judaism is both a religion and a national culture. We firmly believe that history has a purpose, humanity a destiny, and we have a role in shaping the future.

"The Egyptian, the Babylonian, and the Persian rose, filled the planet with sound and splendor, then faded on to dream-stuff and passed away; the Greek and the Roman followed, and made a vast noise, and they are gone; other people have sprung up and held their torch high for a time, but it burned out, and they sit in twilight now, or have vanished. The Jew saw them all, beat them all, and is now what he always was, exhibiting no decadence, no infirmities of age, no weakening of his parts, no slowing of his energies, no dulling of his alert and aggressive mind."
-Mark Twain, Harper, 1899

Just how can two cents have such an implausible impact on the world? I think the answer is simple. Torah! The Jewish people are driven by the challenges of life. We excel because of our passion, our commitment, our drive, and our perseverance to succeed, and Torah is our roadmap, our blueprint for life. Consider the following story:

A new flood is foretold and nothing can be done to prevent it. In three days, the waters will wipe out the world. The greatest leaders of the major religions go on worldwide television to make their final plea.
The leader of Islam reminds the people of their belief in predestination, that God has full knowledge and control over all that occurs.

The leader of Buddhism pleads with everyone to become a Buddhist; that way they will at least find salvation in Heaven.

The Pope goes on television and passionately speaks to the viewing audience, "It is still not too late to accept Jesus."

The Chief Rabbi of Israel approaches the podium, stands silent for what seems to be an eternity, looks directly into the television camera, and slowly but solemnly states, "My people," he pauses, "we have three days to learn to live underwater."

"IMAGINATION IS THE BEGINNING OF CREATION." - Albert Einstein

Though often facing anti-Semitism, both institutional and cultural, the Jewish people have historically responded with innovation and adaptability. Jewish inventors, doctors, economists, and scientists have left their mark over the years with a combination of creative thinking and hard work. From a Teddy Bear and Barbie Doll to an Uzi submachine gun and more, it's amazing how much our two pennies have contributed to the world. How do we measure Jewish achievement? Well, let's consider this informal list of Jewish inventions:

FIRST SOME REALLY BIG INVENTIONS: God, the Atomic Bomb, the Thermonuclear Bomb, Genetic Engineering, the Nuclear Chain Reactor, and Virtual Reality.

NEXT, SOME REALLY PRACTICAL INVENTIONS: Jeans, Lipstick, the Ballpoint Pen, Contraceptives, Instant Coffee, the Sewing Machine, the Television Remote Control, Traffic Lights, Scotchguard, the Flexistraw, and Duracell batteries.

THEN THERE'S OUR CULTURAL CONTRIBUTIONS: Hollywood, the Sit-Com, the Long Playing Record, Woodstock, Sound Movies, Videotape, Color Television,

Instant Photography, Holography, the Barbie Doll, and the Teddy Bear.

OF COURSE WE CANNOT LEAVE OUT THE GAME CHANGERS: Monotheism, Psychoanalysis, the Theory of Relativity, and the Weekend (Shabbat).

AND THEN THERE'S THOSE INVENTIONS BEGINNING WITH THE LETTER "C": Capitalism, Communism, Circumcision, Cheesecake, Cafeterias, the Corvette (nice car), and Chutzpah!

AND SINCE WE'RE ALSO KNOWN NEVER TO BUY RETAIL, WE INVENTED: Discount Stores, Pawn Shops, the Shopping Cart, and the Ready-to-Wear Clothing Industry.

NOW, LET'S ADD THE "I FEEL BETTER ALREADY" CROWD: Prozac, Valium, The Polio Vaccine, Radiation, Chemotherapy, the Artificial Kidney Dialysis Machine, the Defibrillator, the Cardiac Pacemaker, the Vaccination against the deadly "Hepatitis B" virus, and the Vaccinating Needle.

THEN THERE'S CHAI TECH: Google, the Wire Transmission Facsimilie (FAX), the Microphone, the Gramophone, the Microprocessing Chip, Optical Fiber Cable, the Laser, Cellular Technology, and the Videotape Recorder.

AND HOW DID WE LIVE WITHOUT THESE?: Scale Model Electric Trains, the Pager, the Walkie-talkie, Refrigerated Railroad Cars, High-vacuum Electron Tubes, the Incandescent Lamp, Kodachrome Film, the Blimp, the Adding Machine, Stainless Steel, Drip Irrigation, and Tapered Roller Bearings,

But let's push our kvelling a little further. Did you know Israel was the country to develop the USB flash drive, or the Epilady, or the BabySense device, which helps prevent crib deaths by monitoring a baby's breathing and movements through the mattress while they sleep, or an app called Viber, allowing you to make calls across the world for free using Wifi?

And, though it's not an invention, but rather an amazing use of technology, Israel really is 'the land of milk and honey' thanks to its 'super cows', which produce far more milk than other countries. Israeli cows produce up to 10.5 tons a year – 10% more than North American cows and almost 50% more than Germany's cows! A combination of air conditioning, constant monitoring and pedometers to tell when the animals are getting fidgety helps to keep the milk flowing, Go figure!

The Nobel Prize is widely regarded as the most prestigious award available in the fields of literature, medicine, physics, chemistry, physiology, peace, and economics. Between 1901 and 2017, more than 923 Nobel Prizes were handed out. Of these, at least 201 went to Jews, accounting for 23% of all individual recipients worldwide, and constituting 37% of all U.S. recipients during the same period. In the scientific research fields of chemistry, economics, physics, and physiology, the corresponding world and U.S. percentages are 26% and 39%, respectively. Among women laureates in the four research fields, the Jewish percentages (world and U.S.) are 33% and 50%, respectively. Since the turn of the century (i.e., the year 2000), Jews have been awarded 26% of all Nobel Prizes and 28% of those in the scientific research fields.

I know statistics can be boring, but given that Jews comprise less than two cents of the world's population, these numbers are beyond mind-boggling.

We are proud of our GREAT THINKERS, like Albert Einstein, the most famous scientist of the 20th century, whose work laid the foundation for much of modern physics and had a profound impact on everything from quantum theory to nuclear power and the atom bomb; and Karl Marx, the German philosopher, economist, and revolutionary, who influenced modern socialism and all social sciences, and is considered one of the founders of economic history and sociology; and Dr. Sigmund Freud, an Austrian physician, the founder of psychoanalysis and father of psychiatry, whose psychoanalytic theories profoundly influenced 20th-century thought.

In the field of medicine, a significant number of Jews have made medical and scientific advances that are credited with saving billions of lives. Jewish involvement in medicine is legendary, going back at least 800 years to the time of the famous Jewish physician, Maimonides. Some of our HEROES IN SCIENCE AND MEDICINE and their lifesaving contributions include:
Karl Landsteiner - Blood Transfusions
Abel Wolman - Chlorination of Drinking Water
Benjamin Rubin - Smallpox Eradication
Samuel Katz - Measles Vaccine
Paul Ehrlich - Diphtheria and Tetanus Antitoxin, and winner of the Nobel Prize for curing Syphilis
Jonas Salk – Polio Vaccine
Albert Sabin - Polio Pill
Henry Heimlich – the Heimlich Maneuver;
Baruch Blumberg - Vaccine for Hepatitis
Oskar Minkowski – Discovery of Insulin
Casmir Funk, a Polish Jew, who pioneered a new field of medical research and coined the word "Vitamins."

Dr. Simon Baruch performed the first successful operation for Appendicitis.

Briton Epstein identified the first Cancer Virus.

Dr. Abraham Jacobi - America's father of Pediatrics.

When we turn our attention to the LEADERS IN BUSINESS AND FINANCE, we discover Haym Solomon and Isaac Moses were responsible for creating the first modern-banking institutions. And that Jews created the first department stores: the Altmans, Gimbels, Kaufmanns, Lazaruses, Magnins, Mays, and Strausses became leaders of major retailing empires. Isadore & Nathan Straus became the sole owners of Macy's, the world's largest department store, in 1896. Then there's Julius Rosenwald who revolutionized the way Americans purchased goods by improving the Sears Roebuck's mail order merchandising system. The fortunes of English-Jewish financiers such as Isaac Goldsmid, Nathan Rothschild, David Salomons, and Moses Montefiore helped England become an empire, while Armand Hammer (Arm & Hammer), a physician and businessman, originated the largest trade between the United States and Russia. And then there's Levi Strauss who invented durable pants made of a heavy blue denim material (called "genes" in France), that were first used by Forty-niners during the Gold Rush. The pants he created, called Levis or jeans, have become an emblem of the American West and an emissary of the Western lifestyle around the world.

Thanks to the very talented PEOPLE IN THE ENTERTAINMENT INDUSTRY, we celebrate their creativity, giving thanks to those European Jews who were the founding fathers of all the Hollywood Studios. The MGM team of Samuel L. Goldwyn and Louis B. Mayer produced the first full-length sound picture, "The Jazz Singer." Adolph Zukor built the first theater used solely to show motion pictures. Sherry Lansing of Paramount Pictures became the first woman president of a major Hollywood studio. And Steven Spielberg, grateful to all who preceded him in his passion for the movies, became the most successful filmmaker since the advent of film. The world of music burst into song, thanks to George and Ira Gershwin, and Irving Berlin being three of the most prolific composers of the 20th century, while Flo Zigfield ("Zigfield Follies") created American burlesque. In the meantime, Harry Houdini (Weiss) was astounding the world with his magic.

Then there are those who CHAMPIONED THE IMAGINATION OF CREATION THROUGH INVENTION, like Theodor Judah who was the chief architect and engineer for the American Transcontinental railroad. In 1909, four Jews were among the 60 multi-cultural signers of the call to the National Action, which resulted in the creation of the NAACP. One year later, Louis Blaustein and his son opened the first gas station, eventually founding Amoco Oil. Ten years later in Detroit, Max Goldberg opened the first commercial parking lot. And if music was your form of relaxation, Emile Berliner developed the modern-day phonograph, patenting the machine he called the gramophone. Berliner made possible the modern record industry, his company eventually being absorbed by the Victor Talking Machine Company, now known as RCA.

For those with a more sophisticated palate, the world of ART AND LITERATURE was brought to life by Marc Chagall (born Segal, Russia), one of the 20th century's greatest artists. The famous poem of Jewish Poet Emma Lazarus - "give me your tired...your poor...your huddled masses," - appears as the inscription on the Statue of Liberty. And Anne Frank, well, she kept a diary.

Education and critical thinking are embedded in our culture. It would be difficult to name an academic discipline in which the Jewish people have not played a leading role.

Physics: Albert Einstein

Medicine: Jonas Salk, Albert Sabin

Law: Louis Brandeis, Benjamin Cardozo, Felix Frankfurter

Psychology and Psychiatry: Sigmund Freud

Finance: Bernard Baruch

Philosophy: Baruch Spinoza, Maimonides, Karl Marx

With Jewish influence also extending to linguistics, paleontology, anthropology, sociology, economics, mathematics, chemistry (and so very much more), you can see how the world of education has been impacted by our people.

Jewish interest in education, including its advanced forms, goes back to the early days of our people. Historically, Jews have typically been more educated than the average population of the countries in which they have lived. We are expected to read the Torah and teach it to our children.

As a whole, Jews have done very well for themselves in the West since World War II. We are nearly twice as likely to have a college degree as the average American and more than four times as likely to have a graduate degree. Jewish households report a 25% higher income than the average American household. Over 80% of Jewish high school graduates attend college. Although we are only 2% of the American population, more than 20% of students at such Ivy League schools as Harvard, Brown, Columbia, the University of Pennsylvania, Yale, and Cornell, are Jewish.

Being a minority, we chose to concentrate in a few industries and occupations in order to be able to maintain our cohesion and group identity separate from the majority. Because we were often barred from agricultural occupations, the industries and vocational pursuits we chose to specialize in were in cities and were human capital intensive, thus shaping our location and our educational choices.

Jewish Americans are the most powerful and influential ethnic group in America. We comprise 48% of U.S. billionaires. 18% of Jewish households have a net worth of $1 million or more. More than 55% of all Jewish adults received a college degree, and 25% earned a graduate degree. More than 60% of all employed Jews are in one of the three highest status job categories: professional or technical (41%), management and executive (13%) and business and finance (7%). Over 45% of large gifts made to charity are made by Jewish Americans. Over 50% of Jewish Americans live in just four states: New York, New Jersey, Florida and California.

The prestigious Fields Medal is often described as the "Nobel Prize of Mathematics." It is awarded to the world's brightest mathematicians under age 40. One out of every four Fields Medals winners are Jews.

As for the arts, America's leading symphony orchestras have been led by Jewish conductors one-third of the time. We have created nearly two-thirds of Broadway's longest running musicals. Probably one-fourth of the greatest photographers of all time were Jewish, including Joe Rosenthal, whose shot of five Marines raising the flag at Iwo Jima (immortalized by a bronze statue in Arlington National Cemetary), and Alfred Eisenstadt, whose August 1945 Times Square shot of a sailor leaning over to kiss a pretty girl on V-J Day, as well as his shot of Winston Churchill raising two fingers above his head in the shape of a "V" for victory, are instantly recognizable.

Whether it be movie directors earning Oscars (the brainchild of Louis B. Mayer), artistic recognition from the Kennedy Center, or Grammy Lifetime Awards, we play much bigger than our numbers would dictate.

A lot of statistics true, yet you cannot help but wonder how much more we could have contributed if the holocaust had not destroyed 6,000,000 of our number.

LIFE IS TOO SHORT TO WORRY ABOUT MATCHING SOCKS...

While it's true we've overachieved when it comes to the Nobel Prizes for literature, and Pulitzer Prizes for non-fiction, you'll also find us overrepresented in the United States Senate, the House of Representatives, and, since 1917, when Judge Louis Brandeis was appointed to the Supreme Court, members of the highest court in the land.

We were instrumental in the creation of the Federal Reserve System, and have headed it for more than 40 of the last 45 years.

For Jews, with entrepreneurial success comes "tzedakah." With tzedakah comes philanthropy, and with philanthropy comes donating billions and billions (and billions and billions and billions) of dollars to worthwhile causes all over the globe (education, hospitals, science, medical research, the arts, museums, etc.).

We've created whole new industries, and have occupied corner offices as CEOs of some of America's largest companies: Viacom, Google, Oracle, Miramax, Warner Brothers, Dreamworks, Comcast, CBS, MGM, Universal Studios, ABC, 20th Century Fox, Columbia Pictures, Facebook, eBay, Sun Microsystems, Cisco Systems, Häagen-Dazs, Dunkin' Donuts, Baskin Robbins, Toys R Us, Mattel, Wynn Hotels, Ameriquest, Neiman

Marcus, Royal Caribbean Cruise Lines, Levi's, DKNY, Calvin Klein, Home Depot, Kenneth Cole, Loews Corporation, Goldman Sachs, H&R Block, Charles Schwab Corp., Max Factor, Reebok, Chanel, Harley-Davidson, Hoffman-LaRoche, L'Oreal, NewsCorp., MTV, Nickelodeon, Fox Entertainment, Lazard Freres, Polo Ralph Loren, Disney, Sears, Starbucks, Seagram's, Time Warner, NBC, Citigroup, Marvel Entertainment, Microsoft, Dell, Ziff-Davis Publishing, Mirage Resorts, Sotheby's, Hartz Mountain, Revlon, Newhouse Publications, Century 21, Yahoo, Merck, American Airlines, AT&T Cable, Philadelphia Eagles, Progressive Insurance, MBNA Financial, the Wall Street Journal, Estee Lauder, Kraft, Little Caesar's Pizza, The Gap, IAC, Dallas Mavericks, AIG, Carnival Cruise Lines, RCA, MCA, Las Vegas Sands, Slim-Fast, De Beers, Qualcomm, Western Publishing, and John Deere, just to name a few.

We pioneered the ready-to-wear apparel industry. Names like Levi Strauss, Ralph Lauren, Calvin Klein, Donna Karan, Anne Klein, Kenneth Cole, and Isaac Mizrahi, are contemporary representatives of that legacy.

We created the garment industry. We became labor leaders and advocates for the poor and oppressed. In that same era, Samuel Gompers headed organized labor for much of the early twentieth century. Later, others (Abbie Hoffman, Jerry Rubin, Betty Friedan, Gloria Steinem) devoted their lives to social change.

Helena Rubenstein, Estee' Lauder, and Charles Revson pioneered the prestige cosmetics industry.

More than half of America's department stores were started or run by Jews, including such greats as Macy's, Federated, B.Altman's, I. Magnin, F & R Lazarus, Gimbel's, May Company, Bloomingdale's, Filene's,

Saks, Abraham & Straus, Neiman Marcus, and Bergdorf Goodman.

In specialty retailing, major chains such as Gap Stores, Limited, Mervyn's, Barney's, Home Depot, Men's Warehouse, Ritz Camera, and Bed, Bath & Beyond, are all Jewish creations.

In television retailing, both QVC and the Home Shopping Network were largely shaped by Jews. In diamonds (every girl's best friend), DeBeers and Lev Leviev Group are the dominant forces in the worldwide diamond trade, while Zales, Helzbergs, Whitehall, and Friedman's are among the leading diamond and jewelry retailers.

Go on, drink your Starbucks coffee, enjoy your Dunkin' Donuts, go off your diet with a Dove Bar, or some ice cream from H'agen Dazs, Ben & Jerry's, and/or Baskin-Robbins, but then (after you step on the scale), don't forget to sign up for Weight Watchers, Jenny Craig, and NutriSystem programs, or buy some Slim-Fast in the supermarket. All these companies were started by Jewish entrepreneurs.

We may lounge in our Fairmont, Loews, Hyatt, Helmsley, or Wynn hotel, or cruise on any of the magnificent floating resorts of Carnival and Royal Caribbean cruise lines. These companies were also founded and/or largely shaped by Jews.

Every major Hollywood studio except United Artists, was created by Jews (Universal, Paramount, MGM, 20th Century Fox, Warner Bros., RKO), as were NBC and CBS. Of the three original television networks, only ABC was not started by a Jew, but Leonard Goldenson bought it seven years after its founding and ran it for the next 45 years.

Viacom and Comcast were largely created by two Jewish families, while Steve Ross and Gerald Levin played critical roles at Time Warner.

In publishing, America's newspaper of record is the New York Times, and in the nation's capital, the world follows the Washington Post. The Pulitzer Prize is the legacy of the family that still runs the St. Louis Post Dispatch and Arizona Daily Star. Reuters, Newhouse, Triangle and Ziff Davis are just a few of our leading magazine publishers. Random House, Alfred A. Knopf, Simon & Schuster, and Farrar, Straus and Giroux are but four of the major book publishers created and run by Jews.

In finance, the story is much the same. Premier names like Goldman Sachs, Lehman Brothers, and Lazard Freres are just three contemporary names of a legacy dating back to the Rothschilds, Warburgs, Kuhn-Loebs, and Seligmans.

Jews were generally not allowed to own real estate outside the ghetto for the better part of 1800 years. We have compensated by becoming a major force in development and management of property all over the world. Of the five largest Real Estate Investment Trusts listed by Forbes magazine in the last decade, four were headed by Jews.

Michael Bloomberg, once New York City's mayor, created Bloomberg LP, the enterprise that gave him the ability to take on a second career. It is the largest financial information company in the world.

Few people know that the shell of Shell Oil traces back to a London curio shop where the Samuels family featured seashells before two sons started trading kerosene. Nor would they know that the Amoco part of BP Amoco was the creation of the father and son team of Louis and Jacob Blaustein, who also invented the railroad tank car. Amerada Hess, Aurora Oil, Marvin Davis, Occidental Petroleum, and Kaiser-Francis are just a few more members of this "black gold" fraternity started or principally shaped by Jews.

America's great legacy of the Guggenheim Museums, and Smithsonian's Hirschorn Museum and Sculpture Garden, have their origins in the success of two great mining operations established by Jewish families.

In business services, Manpower is the world's largest temporary staffing company, just as ADP is the largest payroll processing company and H&R Block is the largest preparer of tax returns. All started by Jews.

And when it comes to modern technology, we have a Star of David All Star team:

Michael Dell created Dell, the world's largest and most valuable computer company. Sergei Brin co-founded Google, the world's most successful search engine. Steve Ballmer headed Microsoft, the world's largest software company. Lawrence Ellison co-founded and heads Oracle, the world's second largest software company. Andrew Grove co-founded, and served as chairman of the world's dominant microprocessor and memory chip company, Intel. Irwin Jacobs co-founded and heads the communications protocol/chip company, Qualcomm, whose chips are in most U.S. cell phones, and are slated to be utilized in the next generation of cell phones worldwide. Terry Semel, was Chairman and CEO of

Yahoo, Jeffrey Skoll, first employee, and President of E-Bay, and Barry Diller, Chairman and Senior Executive of IAC/Interactive Corp. and the media executive responsible for the creation of Fox Broadcasting Company and USA Broadcasting. As all-star teams go, not too shabby.

Out of the 32 NFL teams, 19 are owned by Jews. 17 out of 30 NBA teams are owned by Jews (in other words, if you're watching an NBA game, there's a 32% chance that both teams are owned by Jews). There are 10 MLB teams owned by Jews. We've also served as commissioners for the major professional sports of baseball, football, basketball, hockey, and soccer.

And when the games have more to do with brains than testosterone, we Jews have held the world chess championship title for roughly two-thirds of the time since it began in 1834, while in bridge, the legend of the game was Charles Goren.

Considering we constitute less than two cents of the world's population, our contributions to religion, science, literature, technology music, medicine, finance, philosophy, and entertainment, is staggering.

In the field of medicine alone, Jewish contributions continue to be so. It was a Jew who created the first polio vaccine, who discovered insulin, who discovered that aspirin dealt with pain, who discovered chloral hydrate for convulsions, who discovered streptomycin, who discovered the origin and spread of infectious diseases, who invented the test for the diagnosis of syphilis, who identified the first cancer virus, who discovered the cure for pellagra, and added to the knowledge about yellow fever, typhoid, typhus, measles, diphtheria and influenza.

Today, Israel, a nation still in its infancy, has emerged at the forefront of stem-cell research, which will, in the near future, give humanity unprecedented medical treatment for degenerative diseases.

Over the past 2000 years, millions of Jews have been killed in Inquisitions, Pogroms, and more recently, the horror of the Holocaust. You can't help but wonder how much more humanity might have gained from the descendants of those murdered and their potential contributions to mankind. Would we already have the cure for Cancer? Or Alzheimer's? Or the common cold? Would we have discovered other intelligent life in the universe? Or even how life began? What about UFO's, or what the universe is made of? How much can the human life span be extended? How did human speech originate? Is there life after death? Is time travel possible? These answers are still waiting to be discovered.

"The resourcefulness of the modern Jew, both in mind and soul, is extraordinary."
Friedrich Nietzsche, German Philosopher

So, how are those two pennies in your hand feeling now? SAY IT LOUD AND SAY IT PROUD.

LO GIUOCO DEL LOTTO D'ITALIA

Bingo originated in Italy in the 14th century. It was known as "Lo Giuoco del Lotto D'Italia." The original Italian version of the game traveled far and wide, eventually finding its way to a carnival in Atlanta, where it was first named 'Beano' not bingo! But it took a Jewish entrepreneur to truly see the potential for this seemingly innocent simple game.

Edwin S. Lowe discovered a group of men playing 'Beano' in the 1920's in Florida. Lowe was so intrigued with the game and how addicted the people playing it seemed to be, when he returned to his home in New York, he purchased some dried beans, some cardboard for cards and rubber stamps for marking. He decided to see if his "gut feeling" was correct, and tested his instincts on his friends. During one of the games, a player close to winning got very excited, and yelled out, "Bingo" rather than "Beano" when her final number was called. Oops.

This is when Edwin S. Lowe had the idea to rename the game "Bingo" and market it as such. He put out two versions of Bingo; a 12-card version that cost one dollar and a 24-card version that cost two dollars.

The game was a huge success. But before he journeyed off to the patent office to unsuccessfully register the Bingo trademark, Lowe showed his game to the parish priest of a Catholic church in Wilkes-Barre, Pennsylvania.

The priest immediately saw the fund raising prospects for such a game.

With the Catholic Church as a ready buyer, Lowe dove headlong into the bingo business. Within a few years, he had 226 presses printing out bingo cards round the clock. By 1934, there were an estimated 10,000 bingo games a week across the United States, and Lowe's firm had 1000 employees trying to keep up with the demand.

Edwin Lowe also invented and marketed a dice game called "Yahtzee". He ultimately sold his company to the Milton Bradley Company of Springfield, Massachusetts, for $26,000,000.

BINGO!

NOW, ABOUT SUPERMAN BEING JEWISH…

Jerry Siegel and Joe Shuster, two misfit teens in Depression era Cleveland, were more like Clark Kent, meek, mild, and myopic, than his secret identity, Superman. Jerry wrote stories, and Joe illustrated them. In 1934, they created a superhero who was everything they were not. It was four more years before they convinced a publisher to take a chance on their Man of Steel in a new format, the comic book.

Superman's creators gave plenty of clues as to his origin. From his Kryptonian name Kal-El (Hebrew for "vessel of God"), to his origin story straight out of Exodus (as with Moses, his parents launched him to safety and adoption by non-Jews, Martha and Jonathan Kent). The rest, as they say, is history. The personal conclusion of this writer, since Superman's creators were Jewish, it stands to reason their brain*child* is also Jewish.

Cartoons, like all mass entertainment, are both a reflection of the society in which they are created, and a creative force with an impact on that society. Jews have been major contributors to American cartoon arts from early in the 20th century to the present day. We've brought our own unique outlooks, influenced by immigration and assimilation, to this craft. Jewish cartoonists helped shape American thought as well as reflecting the values of American Jews. Consider their output......

Ralph Bakshi ("Fritz the Cat," "Lord of the Rings"); Al Capp ("L'il Abner"); Bob Kane ("Batman"); Gil Kane ("Green Lantern"); Jack Kirby ("Captain America"); Mel Lazarus ("Momma," "Miss Peaches"); Stan Lee ("Spiderman," "X-Men," the "Hulk," "Fantastic Four"); Al Feldstein ("Mad Magazine"); Max Fleisher ("Popeye," "Betty Boop"); Friz Freleng ("Looney Tunes").

Now let's add a few social critics, like Jules Pfeiffer, Rube Goldberg, three time Pulitzer Prize winner Herblock, and Al Hirschfeld, caricaturist of the world's most famous celebrities.

Leon Schlesinger was an American film producer, most noted for founding Leon Schlesinger Productions. From the creative minds of this company was born Bugs Bunny, Daffy Duck, Porky Pig, Elmer Fudd, Sylvester, Tweety Bird, Marvin the Martian, the Tazmanian Devil, Wile E. Coyote, Road Runner, Foghorn Leghorn, Yosemite Sam, Pepe LePew, and Speedy Gonzalez. Looney Tunes, which was the title all these American icons worked under, was produced by Leon Schlesinger Productions from 1933 – 1944. Schlesinger then sold his studio to Warner Bros. in 1944, and the newly renamed Warner Bros. Cartoons continued production until 1963.

Moses Koenigsberg, a Hearst executive, founded King Features Syndicate in 1913, and was pivotal in making cartoons influential in American life. Today, King Features distributes about 150 comic strips, newspaper columns, editorial cartoons, puzzles and games, to nearly 5000 newspapers worldwide.

And then there's "Mad Magazine," founded by Harvey Kurtzman, a great satirical magazine (it started as a comic book), full of Jewish expressions, humor and references. Like the films of Mel Brooks, "Mad Magazine" featured Yiddush words in unexpected places, Jewish names on characters, the satirical bite characteristic of much Jewish humor, and was read by millions. And everyone knew "Mad's" mascot, Alfred E. Neuman, a true American icon.

Ever wonder why Curious George is so curious, so fond of travel, so prone to mischief, yet always narrowly escapes disaster? An exhibit at New York's Jewish Museum suggests that curious readers look no further than the real-life adventures of the husband and wife team who created the beloved character. H.A. and Margaret Reys were German Jews living in Paris on the eve of the Nazi invasion. Two days before the Germans marched into Paris, they fled on bicycles, carrying drawings for their picture books, including one about a mischievous monkey. Hans and Margaret created the monkey character that is always on the run while they themselves were on the run. The recurring motif of the monkey's narrow escape from danger is autobiographical.

One final note. What do all these characters have in common? Bugs Bunny, Daffy Duck, Porky Pig, Sylvester the Cat, Tweety Bird, Foghorn Leghorn, Yosemite Sam, Wile E. Coyote, Woody Woodpecker, Barney Rubble, Mr. Spacely, Speed Buggy, Captain Caveman, and Heathcliff.   The voice of a genius, Mel Blanc. Th..th..th..that's all folks!

A ROSE BY ANY OTHER NAME...

Decades ago, Hollywood stars would hide their ethnicity because antisemitism was so rampant. Thus Samuel Goldfish changed his name to Goldwyn and Cecil B. de Mille insisted that he was a Gentile until his death when a Rabbi officiated at his funeral. It is interesting to note that in their personal, off-screen relationships, Hollywood and Broadway performers, producers, and moguls always used their Yiddish given names. It was only from the American public at large that they felt compelled to hide their Jewish identity.

PUBLIC PERSONA	BIRTH CERTIFICATE
Joey Adams	Joseph Abramowitz
Eddie Albert	Eddie Heimberger
Woody Allen	Allen Konigsberg
Harold Arlen	Hyman Arluck
Lauren Bacall	Betty Perske
Jack Benny	Benny Kubelsky
Milton Berle	Milton Berlinger
Irving Berlin	Izzy Baline
George Burns	Nathan Birnbaum
Joan Blondell	Rosebud Blustein
Joyce Brothers	Joyce Bauer
Dorothy Lamour	Dorothy Kaumeyer

Charles Bronson	Charles Buchinsky
Mel Brooks	Melvin Kaminsky
Joey Bishop	Joey Gottlieb
Rona Barrett	Rona Burnstein
Cyd Charisse	Tula Finklea
Tony Curtis	Bernie Schwartz
Dyan Cannon	Samile Friesen
Kirk Douglas	Issur Danielovich
Bob Dylan	Robert Zimmerman
Rodney Dangerfield	Jacob Cohen
Joel Grey	Joel Katz
Elliott Gould	Elliott Goldstein
John Garfield	Jules Garfinkle
George Gershwin	Jacob Gershwine
Paulette Goddard	Marion Levy
Eydie Gorme	Edith Gormezano
Lorne Green	Chaim Leibowiz
Judy Holliday	Judith Tuvin
Leslie Howard	Leslie Steiner
Buddy Hackett	Leonard Hacker
Jill St. John	Jill Oppenheim
Al Jolson	Asa Yoelson
Danny Kaye	David Kaminsky
Alan King	Irwin Kniberg
Larry King	Larry Zeiger
Tina Louise	Tina Blacker
Ann Landers	Esther Friedman
Michael Landon	Eugene Orowitz
Steve Lawrence	Sidney Leibowitz
Hal Linden	Hal Lipshitz
Jerry Lewis	Joseph Levitch
Karl Malden	Maiden Sekulovitch
Ethel Merman	Ethel Zimmerman

Jan Murray   Murray Janofsky
Walter Matthau   Walter Matthow
Lily Palmer   Maria Peiser
Jan Pierce   Pincus Perelmuth
Roberta Peters   Roberta Peterman
Eleanor Parker   Ellen Friedlob
Joan Rivers   Joan Molinsky
Tony Randall   Sidney Rosenberg
Edward G. Robinson   Emanuel Goldenberg
Artie Shaw   Avrohom Arshawsky
Dinah Shore   Frances Rose Schorr
Shelly Winters   Shirley Schrift
Gene Wilder   Jerome Silberman
Bea Arthur   Bernice Frankel
Barbara Bain   Millicent Fogel
Victor Borge   Borge Rosenbaum
Fanny Brice   Fanny Borach
Albert Brooks   Albert Einstein
Lenny Bruce   Leonard Alfred Schneider
Red Buttons   Aaron Chwatt
Eddie Cantor   Edward Israel Iskowitz
Phoebe Cates   Phoebe Katz
Jeff Chandler   Ira Grossel
Andrew Dice Clay   Andrew Silverberg
Lee J. Cobb   Leo Jacobi
Howard Cosell   Howard Cohen
Howard Da Silva   Howard Silverblatt
Melvyn Douglas   Melvyn Hesselberg
Robert Evans   Robert Shapera
Larry Fine   Laurence Feinberg
Brad Garrett   Brad Gerstenfeld
Jack Gilford   Jacob Gellman
Lee Grant   Lyova Haskell Rosenthal

Lawrence Harvey	Laruschka Mischa Skikne
Buck Henry	Buck Henry Zuckerman
Pee Wee Herman	Paul Ruebens
Stephen Hill	Soloman Krakovsk
Curly Howard	Jerome Lester Horwitz
Moe Howard	Moses Horwitz
Shemp Howard	Shemp Horwitz
Sam Jaffe	Shalom Jaffe
David Janssen	David Harold Meyer
Lainie Kazan	Lainie Levine
Shari Lewis	Shari Hurwitz
Peter Lorre	Laszlo Lowenstein
Bill Macy	Wolf Marvin Garber
Chico Marx	Leonard
Groucho Marx	Julius
Gummo Marx	Milton
Harpo Marx	Adolf
Zeppo Marx	Herbert
Elaine May	Elaine Berlin
Paul Muni	Muni Weisenfreund
Winona Ryder	Winona Laura Horowitz
Dick Shawn	Richard Schulefand
Silvia Sidney	Sophie Josow
Phil Silvers	Philip Silversmith
Sophie Tucker	Sophia Abuza
Ed Wynn	Isaiah Edwin Leopold
Selma Blair	Selma Bleitner
Jon Stewart	Jonathan Stuart Leibowitz
Jason Alexander	Jay Greenspan
Robby Benson	Robin Segal
Jane Seymour	Joyce Frankenberg
Barbara Hershey	Barbara Lynn Herzstein
Anson Williams	Anson William Heimlick

Piper Laurie	Rosetta Jacobs
Jackie Mason	Yacov Moshe Maza
Ed Ames	Edmund Dantes Urick
Monty Hall	Monte Halperin
Kitty Carlisle Hart	Catherine Conn
Lillian Roth	Lillian Rutstein
Harold J. Stone	Harold Hochstein
John Houseman	Jacques Haussmann
Ben Blue	Benjamin Bernstein
Gertrude Berg	Tilly Edelstein
Molly Picon	Małka Opiekun
Theda Bara	Theodosia Goodman
Douglas Fairbanks	Douglas Ullman
Natalie Portman	Natalie Hershlag
June Allyson	Ella Geisman

By the early sixties, Jews no longer felt they had to assume artificial identities to achieve success (though some still do: Laura Horowitz a/k/a Wynona Ryder). The Golden Age of American Jewry would be defined as that period during which our people began to feel secure enough to be Jews openly. It was a time of transition. The European Jew who had become the Jewish American was now becoming the American Jew.

BREAK A LEG

From 1925 to 1951, three chaotic decades of depression, war, and social upheaval, Jewish writers brought to the musical stage a powerfully appealing vision of America fashioned through song and dance. It was an optimistic, selectively inclusive America in which Jews could at once lose and find themselves, assimilation enacted onstage and off. The Broadway musical clearly emerged as a form by which many Jewish artists negotiated their entrance into secular American society.

The Broadway musical is a uniquely American art form, and many of its creators and most famous practitioners were Jews, as evidenced by the Gershwin brothers *(Porgy and Bess)*, Oscar Hammerstein *(Oklahoma!, Carousel, South Pacific, The King and I)*, Richard Rogers *(The Sound of Music, The Flower Drum Song)*, Lorenz Hart *(Babes in Arms, The Boys From Syracuse, Pal Joey, On Your Toes)*, Kurt Weill *(The Threepenny Opera)*, Leonard Bernstein *(West Side Story)*, Stephen Sondheim *(Sweeney Todd, Into the Woods)*, John Kander and Fred Ebb *(Cabaret, Chicago)*, Charles Strouse *(Bye Bye Birdie, Annie)*, and Stephen Schwartz *(Godspell, Wicked)*.

One of the most potent ingredients in the early evolution of the American musical was Yiddish theater, where a number of Broadway composers either got their start or found inspiration for their 'American' songs.

Delving into the musical hits of Irving Berlin, Jerome Kern, George and Ira Gershwin, Harold Arlen, Larry Hart, Richard Rodgers and Oscar Hammerstein, among selective others, you often wonder how these Ashkenazi Jews, mostly raised speaking Yiddish in New York City as cantors' sons, welded their particular wit, melancholy and sophistication with the rhythmic richness of American music. In their many beloved hits, e.g., Irving Berlin's *"Alexander's Ragtime Band"* (1911), George Gershwin's *"Rhapsody in Blue"* (1923), Rodgers and Hammerstein's *"Oh, What a Beautiful Morning'"* (1943), these sons of refugees from anti-Semitic rumblings in Europe were conducting a passionate romance with America, a romance that would produce……

Funny Girl, Carousel, Brigadoon, Fiddler On The Roof, My Fair Lady, Peter Pan, Gigi, West Side Story, The Sound of Music, Mame, Pajama Game, Annie, Cabaret, Damn Yankees, Guys And Dolls, Gypsy, Oliver, Show Boat, South Pacific, Porgy and Bess, The King And I, Mary Poppins, Chicago, A Chorus Line, Oklahoma, Godspell, Paint Your Wagon, State Fair, Sunset Boulevard, The Producers, Wonderful Town, Miss Saigon, The Most Happy Fella, Annie Get Your Gun, Finian's Rainbow, Dreamgirls, Beauty And The Beast, Bye Bye Birdie, La Cage Aux Folles, Little Shop of Horrors, Pal Joey, Fame, 42nd Street, A Funny Thing Happened On The Way To The Forum, Hello Dolly, Man Of La Mancha, Strike Up The Band, Ragtime, Sweeney Todd, Threepenny Opera, Les Miserables, Of Thee I Sing, Pippin, Applause, Babes In Arms, Flower Drum Song, Fiorello, How To Succeed In Business Without Really

Trying, On The Town, Rent, Promises Promises, 1776, The Wizard Of Oz, Jekyll And Hyde, On Your Toes, Barnum, A Connecticut Yankee, The Desert Song, Follies, The Goodbye Girl, I Can Get It For You Wholesale, Kiss Of The Spider Woman, Shenandoah, Sweet Charity, Titanic, They're Playing Our Song, Zorba, As Thousands Cheer, Bells Are Ringing, Camelot, Lady Be Good, A Little Night Music, Milk And Honey, The Boys From Syracuse, City Of Angels, Do I Hear A Waltz, Company, Crazy For You, Destry Rides Again, Fanny, Into The Woods, High Button Shoes, Gentlemen Prefer Blondes, Lost In The Stars, One Touch Of Venus, On A Clear Day You Can See Forever, Avenue Q, Sister Act, Once Upon A Mattress, The Student Prince, Mr. Wonderful, Wicked, Call Me Madam, There's No Business Like Show Business, White Christmas, Candide, The Will Rogers Follies, Funny Face, Girl Crazy, Seven Brides For Seven Brothers. Oh, Kay, On the Twentieth Century.

In the era of its soaring triumphs, the Broadway musical saturated popular culture and flavored the air everyone breathed. It flowered for only about a quarter of a century, but during that time its effect was inescapable.

Virtually every great Broadway composer of the 20th century was Jewish (with the major exception of the remarkable Cole Porter).

Few of the shows written by the composers from immigrant families drew on Jewish themes, until Jerry Bock and Sheldon Harnick brought us *Fiddler on the Roof* (1964) that told a specifically and clearly identifiable Jewish story in a hit musical. That same year, Jule Styne wrote the music for Fanny Brice's story in *Funny Girl*. Two years later, *Cabaret,* the musical set in Nazi

Germany debuted. And in 2001, Mel Brooks adapted his screenplay *The Producers f*or the stage, putting postwar neo-Nazis and Hitler himself into dance routines. But it was *"Fiddler"* that flung wide a door that had been opened just a crack in the past.

From Fanny Brice, Irving Berlin, and Jerome Kern, to Barbra Streisand, Alan Menken, and Tony Kushner, Jewish performers, composers, lyricists, directors, choreographers and producers have made an indelible mark on Broadway for more than a century, playing an enormous role in creating and shaping that distinctive and distinguished New York cultural institution known as "the Great White Way."

So, thank you, Irving Berlin, Lorenz Hart, Richard Rodgers, Betty Comden, Adolph Green, Jule Styne, Alan Jay Lerner, Frederick Lowe, Cy Coleman, Howard Ashman, Alan Menken, Marvin Hamlisch, Stephen Sondheim, Leonard Bernstein, Oscar Hammerstein II, Ira Gershwin, George Gershwin, Richard Adler, Jerry Ross, Sigmund Romberg, Jerry Bock, Stephen Schwartz, Frank Loesser, Jerry Herman, Kurt Weill, Mel Brooks, Hal David, Burt Bacharach, Jerome Kern, Dorothy Fields, Carol Bayer Sager, Harold Arlen, Richard and Robert Sherman, Sammy Cahn, Claude-Michel Schonberg, and Dorothy Fields, whose musical genius provided inspiration, comfort, and a link to the soul of a nation. And of course, we'd be remiss not to thank their mothers, too.

The Antoinette Perry Award for Excellence in Theatre, more commonly known as the "Tony," recognizes achievement in live American theatre, and is considered the highest U.S. theatre honor. Three of every four Tony Awards for best original score of a musical, and best musical production has been won by Jews.

And if you head west to Hollywood, and the land of "Oscar" (the equivalent of the "Tony"), the Academy Award for best musical scoring of a motion picture, and best original song, here again the majority of recipients of these awards are Jews.

Music is a very large part of our planet's DNA. It's a universal language everyone can enjoy. It inspires, soothes, excites, and provides a common denominator for people of all ages and from all walks of life. It's an important part of the human experience. It can also be just pure entertainment, thanks to Neil Diamond, Bob Dylan, Carole King, Melissa Manchester, Barry Manilow, Randy Newman, Carol Bayer Sager, Billy Joel, Arlo Guthrie, Paul Simon, Art Garfunkel, Carly Simon, Neil Sedaka, Mel Torme, Barbra Streisand, Marvin Hamlisch, Michael Bolton, Richard and Robert Sherman, Hal David, Elmer Bernstein, David Rose, Alan Mencken, Andre Previn, Dmitri Tiomkin, Arthur Freed, Paula Abdul, Harry Chapin, Herb Alpert, Lesley Gore, Steely Dan, Herbie Mann, and the Mamas & the Papas.

The spirit of Christmas is universal ("Ho Ho Ho"), it's essence unquestionably religious. However, if you look at a list of the most popular Christmas songs, you'll find... *The Christmas Song" ("Chestnuts Roasting on An Open Fire"), "Rudolph the Red Nosed Reindeer," "Santa Baby," "Do They Know It's Christmas?" "Holly Jolly Christmas," "Santa Claus Is Coming To Town," "I'll Be Home For Christmas," "Silver Bells," "Winter Wonderland," "It's the Most Wonderful Time of the*

Year," "Sleigh Ride," "Let It Snow! Let It Snow! Let It Snow!" "There's No Place Like Home for the Holidays," "Rockin' Around the Christmas Tree," and *"White Christmas,"* were all written by Jewish songwriters.

God gave Moses (and Mel Brooks) the Ten Commandments. Irving Berlin gave us *"White Christmas"* and *"Easter Parade"*. We gave the world *"Dreidel, Dreidel, Dreidel."*

Music reflects the voices of its generation. It washes away from the soul the dust of everyday life.

DID YOU KNOW?

Born in Bavaria in 1845, Isidor Straus came to the United States at the age of nine, residing first in Georgia and then in New York City. Together with his brother Nathan, they started to sell glassware and china in R. H. Macy's in 1873. By 1896, the enterprise was so successful that the Straus brothers purchased the entire store, helping to build what would become the largest store chain in the world.

Traveling back from a winter in Europe, Isidor and his wife Ida were passengers on the Titanic, when, on the night of April 14, 1912, it hit an iceberg. Although Isidor was offered a seat in a lifeboat to accompany Ida, he refused seating while there were still women and children aboard, and refused to be made an exception. Ida refused to leave Isidor and would not get into a lifeboat without him. She insisted her newly hired English maid, Ellen Bird, get into the lifeboat. She gave Ellen her fur coat, stating she would not be needing it. Ida is reported to have said, "I will not be separated from my husband. As we have lived, so will we die, together." Isidor and Ida were last seen on deck arm in arm. Eyewitnesses described the scene as a "most remarkable exhibition of love and devotion." Both died on April 15th when the ship sank at 2:20 am. Over 40,000 people attended the couple's memorial service.

Contrary to popular opinion, it was not Queen Isabella's jewelry, but Spanish Jewry that made Columbus' historical trip of discovery possible. Actually it was Luis de Santangel, whose grandfather had converted from Judaism to Christianity under pressure of Spanish persecutions, who lent nearly 5 million maravedis (Spanish coins of gold) to pay for the voyage. In addition, Santangel's influence with King Ferdinand and Queen Isabella was decisive in gaining their acceptance of Columbus' proposals. In recognition of his assistance, Santangel was the first to hear of the historic discoveries directly in a personal letter from Columbus.

The first group of Sephardi and Ashkenazi Jewish settlers arrived in New Amsterdam in September, 1654, following their escape from the onslaught of the Inquisition in Recife, Brazil. But they did not receive a warm welcome in Dutch New Amsterdam. Peter Stuyvesant tried to refuse haven to the penniless refugees, and protested to the Dutch West India Company against the "deceitful race" who professed an "abominable religion." Fortunately he was overruled, thanks to the influence of some of the directors of the Company who were Jewish.

Uriah Phillips Levy was barely fourteen years old when he embarked on his naval career by signing on as a cabin boy. Seven years later he volunteered for service in the United States Navy during the War of 1812, "as proof of love to my country." The next year Uriah was captured and imprisoned by the British until the end of the war. In the years following, he faced persecution from many naval officers, had to defend himself in a duel, and was subjected to a total of six court-martials, believed to be instigated by anti-Semitism. It was Levy's wish that he be remembered for his singular efforts to abolish the barbarous punishment of flogging in the U.S. Navy, which resulted in Congressional approval of an anti-flogging bill in 1850.

Uriah Phillips Levy regarded Thomas Jefferson as "one of the greatest men in history," who did much to mold the Republic in a form in which man's religion does not make him ineligible for political or governmental life. Thus, about ten years after the former President's death in 1826, Levy purchased Jefferson's run down estate that was virtually in ruin. He began a long and costly program of renovation and restoration, including the purchase of an additional 2,500 acres adjoining the historic property. After Levy's death in 1862, his will directed that Monticello, the house and property, be left "to the people of the United States."

Levi Strauss was seventeen years old when he emigrated from Bavaria to New York in 1847. He worked for his two brothers, peddling clothing and household items throughout towns and villages in rural New York and Kentucky. Spurred by exciting tales of opportunities for instant wealth in the Gold Rush country of California, Levi Strauss sailed to San Francisco on a clipper ship in 1850, loaded with canvas for tents and wagons. But after a short visit to the gold country, he realized there was a better use for the durable material. He took his unsold canvas to a tailor and had it fashioned into overalls. He later switched from canvas to a tough cotton fabric loomed in Nimes, France, called serge de Nimes (e.g. denim). Today Levi Strauss & Co. is one of the largest apparel manufacturers in the world. The company's motto "Everyone knows his first name" refers to the fact that Levi's® has entered the world's vocabulary as a generic term for blue-jeans.

In 1883, a Pedestal Art Loan Exhibition was held to raise funds for the Statue of Liberty's pedestal. Walt Whitman, Mark Twain, and others contributed original manuscripts, but the highest bid of $1,500 was received for a sonnet "The New Colossus" written just a few days earlier. The immortal words were penned by young Emma Lazarus, soon after her return from a European trip where she had seen the persecution of Jews and others first hand: "Give me your tired, your poor, your huddled masses yearning to breathe free, the wretched refuse of your teeming shore, send these, the homeless, tempest-tossed to me. I lift my lamp beside the golden door." It was not until 1888 that the Statue of Liberty assumed her majestic place in New York's harbor. Sadly, Emma Lazarus didn't witness this historical event since she died of cancer a year earlier, when she was only thirty-eight years old.

While Adolph Ochs' formal education was sketchy, he described his work at the Knoxville (Tennessee) Chronicle as his "high school and university." Beginning as office boy in 1869 at the age of eleven, he was soon promoted to delivery boy at a weekly salary of $1.50. From that time until his death, Ochs never left the newspaper business. He was a founder of the Southern Associated Press and its chairman from 1891 to 1894, and for 35 years he served as a director of the Associated Press. At the age of thirty-eight, Ochs took on the monumental task of reviving the financially ailing New York Times. He insisted on a clean, upright and impartial approach to the news. After only three years of his dynamic leadership, the Times was showing a profit. Ochs purchased a controlling interest in 1900. Starting with a circulation of 9,000, the New York Times at the time of his death sold almost a half million copies daily and nearly three-quarters of a million copies each Sunday. He had made it one of the greatest newspapers in the world.

Henrietta Szold was born in Baltimore, Maryland in 1860, a little more than a year after her parents arrived from Hungary. Her father, a prominent rabbi, gave Henrietta the attention and education usually reserved for an eldest son. She learned German, English, French and Hebrew. In 1909, Ms. Szold first visited Palestine. During her tour she was impressed both by the beauty of the land and the misery and disease among the people. And so, with the support of Rabbi Judah L. Magnes, she formed Hadassah in 1912. Within a year, the fledgling organization had two American nurses in Jerusalem. Today, Hadassah's great hospitals in Jerusalem are world famous, treating over 25,000 patients and handling over 1.5 million medical tests annually, Jews and Arabs alike.

The Henrietta Szold-Hadassah School of Nursing has trained over 1,500 nurses, and the Hebrew University-Hadassah Medical School has graduated more than 1,300 doctors. In 1933, at the age of seventy-three, Henrietta Szold embarked on a major new project, rescuing Jewish children from the oncoming Holocaust. Despite obstacles in dealing with the British Mandate government in

Palestine, by 1948 her Youth Aliya program brought 30,000 children from troubled Europe to Palestine.

The Leica Freedom Train was a rescue effort in which hundreds of Jews were smuggled out of Nazi Germany before the Holocaust by Ernst Leitz of the Leica Camera Company, and his daughter Elsie Kuehn-Leitz. To help his Jewish workers and colleagues, Leitz quietly established what has become known among historians of the Holocaust as the "Leica Freedom Train," a covert means of allowing Jews to leave Germany in the guise of Leitz employees being assigned overseas. Employees, retailers, family members, even friends of family members were "assigned" to Leitz sales offices in France, Britain, Hong Kong and the United States. Leitz's activities intensified after the Kristallnacht of November 1938, during which synagogues and Jewish shops were burned across Germany. German "employees" disembarking from the ocean liner Bremen at a New York pier went to Leitz's Manhattan office, where they were helped to find jobs. The "Leica Freedom Train" was at its height in 1938 and early 1939, delivering groups of refugees to New York City every few weeks until the invasion of Poland on Sept. 1, 1939, when Germany closed its borders. Leitz's daughter, Elsie Kuhn-Leitz, was imprisoned by the Gestapo after she was caught at the border, helping Jewish women cross into Switzerland. She eventually was freed. She also fell under suspicion when she attempted to improve the living conditions of 700 to 800 Ukrainian slave laborers, all of them women, who had been assigned to work in the plant during the 1940s. After the war, Elsie Kuhn-Leitz received numerous honors for her humanitarian efforts, among them the Officier d'honneur des Palmes Academiques from France in 1965, and the Aristide Briand Medal from the European Academy in the 1970s. The Leitz family wanted no publicity for its heroic efforts. Only after the last member of the Leitz family was dead did the "Leica Freedom Train" finally come to light.

Israel Isadore Baline was five when his family fled Russia for the United States after a bloody pogrom. It was an event the boy never forgot. He always remembered the day he arrived in his new homeland, feeling not a sense of relief as "we stood there in our Jew clothes," he said, but with a new sense of fear. The fear of being an outsider in a new world. With other Jewish composers, Irving Berlin helped make the Broadway musical a singularly American art form. In 1924, songwriter Jerome Kern observed "Irving Berlin has no place in American music. He is American music." Berlin's songs include America's unofficial national anthem "God Bless America," as well as perennial standards "Easter Parade" and "White Christmas," plus about 1,500 more for which he wrote both the music and lyrics. Irving Berlin was honored in 1944 by the National Conference of Christians and Jews for "advancing the aims of the conference to eliminate religious and racial conflict." Five years later, he was honored by the New York YMHA as one of "12 outstanding Americans of the Jewish faith." And in recognition of the song "God Bless America," Mr. Berlin was presented with a special Congressional gold medal in 1954 by President Eisenhower. Not bad for a poor immigrant who had only two years of formal schooling and who never learned to read or write music!

When George Gershwin found a defining musical link between the Jewish "wail" and black spirituals, it was more than just a musical affinity. Jews and blacks shared a sense of being outsiders, and the reason their musical idioms form the basis of what we consider quintessential American music, is that we are a nation of outsiders, founded by Europeans, and over the centuries serving as a melting pot of humanity from other countries and cultures. The songs of that experience are the songs of America.

George Gershwin wrote his first songs while working as a pianist with a music publishing firm. He was equally at home writing "pop" tunes, such as "Swanee," "The Man I Love," "S Wonderful," and "I Got Rhythm;" musical comedies like "Oh Kay," "Girl Crazy," and "Of Thee I Sing"; serious music: "Rhapsody in Blue," and "An American in Paris;" and he even pioneered in creating a genuine American folk opera: "Porgy and Bess." Most of the lyrics for his songs were written by his brother Ira. Tragically George Gershwin did not live to be 40, but his music will live forever.

"West Side Story" was originally conceived as a Romeo and Juliet love story with a Jewish gang at war with racist New York homeboys. Jerome Robbins initially proposed that the plot focus on the rivalry between an Irish American family and a Jewish family living on the Lower East Side during the Easter-Passover season. The girl had survived the Holocaust and emigrated from Israel. The conflict was to be centered round the anti-Semitic prejudice of the Catholic "Jets" towards the Jewish "Emeralds." That's not exactly how things worked out. "East Side Story" (the show's original title) became

"West Side Story," and Maria went from Holocaust survivor to the Puerto Rican version of Juliet. The anti-Semitic theme was replaced by a turf war between the "Sharks" and the "Jets." The entire creative team was Jewish, with a script by Arthur Laurents, music by Leonard Bernstein, lyrics by Stephen Sondheim and choreography by Jerome Robbins.

Ray Stark, Fannie Brice's son-in-law, had commissioned an authorized biography of the star based on taped recollections she had dictated, but was unhappy with the result. Stark then turned to Ben Hecht to write the screenplay for a biopic, but neither Hecht nor the ten writers who succeeded him were able to produce a version that satisfied Stark. Finally, Isobel Lennart submitted "My Man," which pleased both Stark and Columbia Pictures executives, who offered Stark $400,000 plus a percentage of the gross for the property.

After reading the screenplay, Mary Martin contacted Stark and proposed it be adapted for a stage musical. Stark discussed the possibility with producer David Merrick, who suggested Jule Styne and Stephen Sondheim compose the score. Sondheim told Styne," You need someone ethnic for the part." Shortly after, Martin lost interest in the project and backed out.

Merrick discussed the project with Jerome Robbins, who gave the screenplay to Anne Bancroft. She agreed to play Brice if she could handle the score. She listened to the score, then stated, "I want no part of this. It's not for me." With Bancroft out of the picture, Eydie Gormé was considered, but she agreed to play Brice only if her husband Steve Lawrence was cast as Nick Arnstein. Since they thought he was wrong for the role, Stark and

Robbins approached Carol Burnett, who said, "I'd love to do it, but what you need is a Jewish girl."

With options running out, Styne thought Barbra Streisand, whom he remembered from *I Can Get It for You Wholesale,* would be perfect. She was performing at the Bon Soir in Greenwich Village and Styne urged Robbins to see her. He was impressed and asked her to audition. Styne later recalled, "She looked awful. All her clothes were out of thrift shops. I saw Fran Stark (Fannie Brice's daughter), staring at her, obvious distaste on her face." Despite his wife's objections, Ray Stark hired Streisand on the spot. And the rest, as they say, is history.

When it came time to cast the screen adaptation, Streisand was Stark's first and only choice to portray Brice onscreen. Columbia Pictures wanted Shirley MacLaine but Stark insisted if Streisand were not cast, he would not allow the film to be made at all. Streisand went on to share the best actress Oscar with Katharine Hepburn ("Lion in Winter"). Streisand's first comment when handed the Oscar statuette was "Hello, handsome."

That line ("Hello, handsome."), was repeated by Max Bialystock in Mel Brooks' musical, *The Producers*. The title of Max's latest flop in that film was "Funny Boy," a musical adaptation of "Hamlet." Brooks also satirized Florence Ziegfield's style of musical extravaganza and use of busty showgirls in his famed staging of the notoriously tasteless and hilariously offensive song, "Springtime for Hitler."

Known as the "master builder" of mid-20th century New York City, Long Island, Rockland County, and Westchester County, Robert Moses was one of the most polarizing figures in the history of urban planning in the United States. His decisions favoring highways over public transit helped create the modern suburbs of Long Island and influenced a generation of engineers, architects, and urban planners who spread his philosophies across the nation. From the 1930s to the 1960s, Robert Moses was responsible for the construction of the Throgs Neck Bridge, the Bronx-Whitestone Bridge, the Henry Hudson Bridge, and the Verrazano-Narrows Bridge, in New York City. His other projects included the Brooklyn-Queens Expressway, the Staten Island Expressway, the Cross-Bronx Expressway, the Belt Parkway, the Laurelton Parkway, Northern State Parkway, Southern State Parkway, the Long Island Expressway, FDR Drive, the Henry Hudson Parkway, and the world famous Jones Beach State Park on the south shore of Long Island. Now there's a bunch of LEGO projects for the ambitious.

Hank Greenberg joined the Detroit Tigers in 1933, and helped them win their first American League pennant in 25 years. The Tigers were champions again the following year, and Hank Greenberg won the American League's Most Valuable Player award by a unanimous vote of the Baseball Writers Association. He won it again in 1940. After Hank Greenberg declined to play in an important game on Yom Kippur in 1934, Edgar Guest published a poem, the last lines of which are: *"We shall miss him on the infield and shall miss him at the bat, but he's true to his religion, and I honor him for that."* As the first Jewish baseball star, Hank Greenberg had to handle racial slurs from fans and opponents alike. Birdie Tebbetts, a Detroit teammate of Greenberg's for seven seasons, recalled that,

"There was nobody in the history of the game who took more abuse than Greenberg, unless it was Jackie Robinson."

The discovery of high-grade silver-lead ore in the Guggenheim mines in Leadville, Colorado in 1881 became the foundation for the Guggenheim fortune. Thus was born the Colorado Smelting and Refining Company. By 1901 the Guggenheims added the American Smelting and Refining Company (ASARCO) to their holdings, becoming the dominant force in the mining industry for the next three decades. Through ASARCO, Kennecott Copper and other family-owned companies, the Guggenheims mined tin in Bolivia, gold in the Yukon, diamonds and rubber in the Belgian Congo, diamonds in Angola, and copper in Alaska, Utah, and Chile, amassing enormous wealth through their mining enterprises.

Solomon R. Guggenheim began using his wealth collecting art in the 1890s, and after World War I, he retired from his business to pursue full-time art collecting. Today, the Guggenheim Museums welcome millions of visitors in New York City, Bilboa, Spain, Berlin, Germany, Venice, Italy, and Abu Dhabi.

Joseph Herman Hirshhorn made his fortune in the mining and oil business. In the 1930s, he focused much of his attention on gold and uranium mining prospects in Canada. In the 1950s, he and geologist Franc Joubin were primarily responsible for the "Big Z" uranium discovery in northeastern Ontario. By 1960, when he sold the last of his uranium stock, he had made over $100 million in cash from the uranium business. When Hirshhorn began to make money, he began to buy art, amassing a collection of paintings and sculptures from the 19th and 20th centuries. He subsequently donated much of his collection, consisting of 6,000 paintings and sculptures (and constituting one of the world's largest private art treasures), to the United States government, along with a $2 million endowment. The Smithsonian Institution established the Joseph H. Hirshhorn Museum and Sculpture Garden in Washington, D.C. in 1966 to hold the collection (the museum opened in 1974). At Hirshhorn's death in 1981, he willed an additional 6,000 works and a $5 million endowment to the museum. Notable artists in the collection include Pablo Picasso, Henry Moore, Jackson Pollock, Francis Bacon, and Willem de Kooning. Outside the museum is a sculpture garden, featuring works by artists Auguste Rodin, David Smith, Alexander Calder, and Jeff Koons.

According to a 2009 PBS documentary, "apart from the atomic bomb, America's greatest fear was polio." As a result, scientists were in a frantic race to find a way to prevent or cure the disease. In 1938, President Franklin D. Roosevelt, the world's most recognized victim of the disease, had founded the National Foundation for Infantile Paralysis (now known as the March of Dimes Foundation), an organization that would fund the development of a vaccine.

In 1947, Dr. Jonas Salk accepted an appointment to the University of Pittsburgh School Of Medicine. In 1948, he undertook a project funded by the National Foundation for Infantile Paralysis to determine the number of different types of polio virus. Salk saw an opportunity to extend this project towards developing a vaccine against polio, and, together with the skilled research team he assembled, devoted himself to this work for the next seven years. The field trial set up to test the Salk vaccine was the most elaborate program of its kind in history, involving 20,000 physicians and public health officers, 64,000 school personnel, and 220,000 volunteers. Over 1,800,000 school children took part in the trial. When news of the vaccine's success was made public on April 12, 1955, Jonas Salk was hailed as a "miracle worker" and the day almost became a national holiday. Around the world, an immediate rush to vaccinate began, with countries including Canada, Sweden, Denmark, Norway, West Germany, the Netherlands, Switzerland, and Belgium planning to begin polio immunization campaigns using Salk's vaccine.

Jonas Salk campaigned for mandatory vaccinations, claiming that public health should be considered a "moral commitment." His sole focus had been to develop a safe and effective vaccine as rapidly as possible, with no interest in personal profit. When asked who owned the patent to it, Salk said, "There is no patent. Could you patent the sun?"

Barbra Streisand is a legend. She is the only artist ever to have earned the Oscar, Tony, Emmy, Grammy, Golden Globe, Cable Ace, and Peabody Awards. She won the 1968 Academy Award for Best Actress in her motion picture debut *(Funny Girl),* and was awarded her second Oscar in 1976 for composing the song "Evergreen" for her hit film, *A Star is Born.* She was awarded a special Tony as "Star of the Decade," and 10 Golden Globes for acting, directing, producing, songwriting, and as World Film Favorite. Barbra Streisand has achieved more gold (37), platinum (21), and multi-platinum (10) albums than any other artist.

Marcel Marceau was a Holocaust hero. He was born Marcel Mangel on March 22, 1923, in Strasbourg, Alsace. His father Charles, was a kosher butcher who loved the arts. Marcel's mother Anne nee Werzberger, took him to a Charlie Chaplin movie when he was five. He was entranced. At the beginning of WWII, he and his brother, Alain, hid their Jewish origins, and changed their name from Mangel to Marceau. His father died in Auschwitz. His mother survived the war. The French Resistance was headed up by many Jews. Marcel and Alain joined the Resistance in Limoges. The Jewish children had to be protected from both the French police and the Germans. Although he was trilingual, Marcel taught hundreds of Jewish children the art of communicating in mime because it was important for the children to converse silently. The children were brought to safety by Marceau in Switzerland. In 1944, he joined the Free French Forces under General Charles de Gaulle, acting as liaison officer to General Patton's army.

Marceau entertained thousands of US troops after the liberation of Paris. He was "discovered" by Laurel and Hardy. He spoke only once in a performance, in Mel Brooks' film *Silent Movie,* and the only word he spoke was "No." His career lasted over 60 years as an actor, director, teacher, interpreter, and public multilingual speaker on five continents. He died on Yom Kippur in 2007.

"Do not the most moving moments of our lives find us without words?"

~Marcel Marceau

The Associated Press reported that newly released tapes from President Lyndon Johnson's White House office showed LBJ's "personal and often emotional connection to Israel." The news agency pointed out that during the Johnson presidency (1963-1969), "the United States became Israel's chief diplomatic ally and primary arms supplier." Historians have revealed that Johnson, while serving as a young congressman in 1938 and 1939, arranged for visas to be supplied to Jews in Warsaw, and oversaw the apparently illegal immigration of hundreds of Jews through the port of Galveston, Texas.

He inherited his concern for the Jewish people from his family. His aunt, Jessie Johnson Hatcher, was a member of the Zionist Organization of America, and had nurtured LBJ's commitment to befriending Jews for 50 years. In 1938, Johnson was told of a young Austrian Jewish musician who was about to be deported from the United States. With an element of subterfuge, LBJ sent him to the U.S. Consulate in Havana to obtain a residency permit, Erich Leinsdorf, the world famous musician and conductor, credited LBJ for saving his life.

During World War II Johnson raised a substantial sum of money for arms to Jewish underground freedom fighters in Palestine, secretly shipping those arms in heavy crates labeled 'Texas Grapefruit.' On June 4, 1945, Johnson visited Dachau. Lady Bird later recalled that when her husband returned home, "he was still shaken, stunned, terrorized, and bursting with an overpowering revulsion and incredulous horror at what he had seen."

Johnson's concern for the Jewish people continued through his presidency. Soon after taking office in the aftermath of John F. Kennedy's assassination in 1963, Johnson told an Israeli diplomat, "You have lost a very great friend, but you have found a better one." Kennedy was the first president to approve the sale of defensive U.S. weapons to Israel, specifically Hawk anti-aircraft missiles. But Johnson approved tanks and fighter jets, all vital after the 1967 war when France imposed a freeze on sales to Israel. Israel won the 1967 war, and Johnson worked to make sure it also won the peace.

The crafting of UN Resolution 242, calling for secure and recognized boundaries after the war, was done under LBJ's scrutiny. In historical context, the American emergency airlift to Israel in 1973, the constant diplomatic support, the economic and military assistance, and the strategic bonds between the two countries can all be credited to the seeds planted by LBJ. His friendship with leading Zionists, his belief that America had a moral obligation to bolster Israeli security and his conception of Israel as a frontier land much like his home state of Texas, President Johnson firmly pointed American policy in a pro-Israel direction.

SAY IT LOUD AND SAY IT PROUD!

A.S. Winston

FASHION IS THE SIGN LANGUAGE OF COMMUNICATION

Before the Civil War, most Americans wore hand-sewn clothes made at home. But in the mid-1800s, Isaac Singer and the sewing machine washed upon the American landscape. Suddenly, mass production of clothes in standardized sizes was within grasp. Dry goods stores, many of them owned by German Jewish immigrants, rushed to capitalize on the opportunity. The country was on the move, expanding South and West in a migration of people and commerce that gave new definition to the term pioneer and new weight to the gods of convenience. By 1890, most Americans were buying their clothes ready-made in shops or ordering them from the Sears Catalogue. And by the turn of the century, 60% of all the Jews employed in New York made their living in the garment industry. It was one of those paradigm-shifting moments in history.

Simply put, to come to New York City in the 1890s with a background in dressmaking or sewing, was a stroke of extraordinary good fortune. It would be like showing up in Silicon Valley in 1986 with ten thousand hours of computer programming already under your belt.

In America clothes were an elixir. Here was a country where image was king, where even if you spoke no English, you could look the part, where a newcomer could go from immigrant to Yankee just by changing clothes.

Within a few years of their arrival, Jewish immigrants dominated the garment industry, and Isaac Singer's sewing machine meant production of more clothes at far greater speed than ever.

From the beginning, the connective tissue of Jewish history in the rag trade was family. The thread that stretches from Levi Strauss to Isaac Mizrahi, from union laborers to runway designers, is made of 'mishpucha.' For all the glitter of the runway, the rag trade is a family business, and Jews were soon hiring Jews to produce and sometimes even design the clothes of the 20th Century.

By 1915, the clothing trade was America's third largest industry, behind only steel and oil. Jews largely created the American clothing production industry, and by the 1920s, they achieved almost exclusive control of it.

More recently, Jews have dominated the fashion aspects of the clothing industry, founding everything from Guess, Gitano, Jordache, Calvin Klein, and Levi-Strauss jeans, to Ralph (Lifshitz) Lauren cosmetics.

Ralph Lauren's success was a template for a generation of Jewish designers who put American style on the fashion map in the years after World War II. Freed from Paris' lock on style, empowered by a baby boom generation of consumers, Anne Klein, Judith Leiber, Ralph Lauren, Calvin Klein, Diane von Furstenberg, Donna Karan, Kenneth Cole and Michael Kors burst on the scene in the 1960s and 1970s, remaking fashion in the image of their times. After them came a new generation,

Marc Jacobs, Isaac Mizrahi, and Zac Posen, who in the 1990s and 2000s, helped democratize luxury, all but ending the business of 'haute couture.'

Most of the designers see little connection between their religious roots and their fashion inspirations. But all of them owe something to the Jews who came before, ancestors who never saw the inside of an English country estate or watched a parade of rail-thin beauties sashay down the runway. Generations of czars and emperors in Europe over the centuries had stripped Jews of their connection to the land, restricting them to work as tailors or peddlers or bankers. Their very existence depended on their acumen at reading the needs and desires of the larger culture. That antenna for "what would play," an accident of historic discrimination, was the distinct advantage that smoothed their journey in fashion from worker bee to trendsetter.

Adrian (born Adrian Greenberg) became the first major costume designer in Hollywood, helping a generation of Jewish immigrant moguls define glamour. A favorite of the stars, Adrian set new standards in movie creativity by dressing the characters in the 1939 classic *The Wizard of Oz,* including the film's signature red-sequined ruby slippers.

As Adrian was designing for Greta Garbo and Norma Shearer in Hollywood, a few Jewish designers in New York were also gaining national fame.

Hattie Carnegie was born in Austria as Henrietta Kanangeiser and decided in America to take the name of the country's most famous industrialist. From her own boutique, Hattie designed colorful dresses and artful jewelry for actresses Joan Crawford and Tallulah Bankhead, and political figures Clare Booth Luce, and the Duchess of Windsor. She also employed a number of seamstresses, like Calvin Klein's grandmother Molly, who taught the future design star to sew.

Sally Milgrim was a favorite of Eleanor Roosevelt, who hired her to design the light blue gown she wore to her husband's first Inaugural Ball in 1933. Known for the quality of her clothes and accessories at a time when most ready-to-wear items were anything but, she also became a favorite of actresses Ethel Merman and Mary Pickford.

Austrian-born Nettie Rosenstein, dubbed by Life Magazine as "among the handful of American dress designers who compete successfully with Paris," designed both of Mamie Eisenhower's inaugural gowns. In an era when department stores insisted on putting their label on the clothes, Rosenstein convinced Bergdorf Goodman and I. Magnin to carry her line under her own label.

Widowed at an early age, Lena Himmelstein Bryant supported herself and her young son as a dressmaker. Borrowing $300 from her brother-in-law, Bryant went to the bank to open an account. The bank officer misspelled her name on the application as Lane instead of Lena. In 1904, she rented a small storefront on Fifth Avenue with living quarters in the back for $12.50 a month. There she hung her garments from the gas fixtures, and opened the doors. Asked by one of her pregnant customers to design something "presentable but comfortable" to wear in public, Bryant created a dress with an elasticized waistband and accordion-pleated skirt. This would be the first known commercially made maternity dress, which soon became the best-selling garment in Bryant's shop. Bryant saw another need just before World War I, noting there were no mass manufacturers of clothing for "stout-figured" women. After measuring 4,500 of her own customers, as well as gathering information from about 200,000 other women, Bryant met the challenge with great success. As of 2013, there were 812 Lane Bryant stores in 46 U.S. states (only Alaska, Hawaii, Montana and Wyoming do not have Lane Bryant stores).

For all the early fame of the pre-war designers, it was really the design aftermath of World War II that served as a seminal divide in the fashion history. Enter the new generation of American fashion powerhouses, many of them Jewish.

Anne Klein was the first, and a visionary. In 1948, at the age of 25, the New York-born Hannah Golofski launched "Junior Sophisticates," creating a new category of clothing in a field that was until then defined as men's, women's and children's. Gearing her designs to a new generation of younger, slimmer girls, she offered a sportier, more casual look. She pioneered the concept of mix-and-match separates to a profession that usually sold clothes in matched sets.

Ralph Lauren launched his first Polo store in 1967, which made only ties. In time, he would become the single richest fashion designer on the planet whose worth exceeded $4 billion. He partnered with the United States Olympic Committee to become an Official Outfitter of the U.S. Olympic Team, for the 2008 Summer Olympics in Beijing, 2010 Winter Olympics in Vancouver, 2012 Summer Olympics in London, 2014 Winter Olympics in Sochi and 2016 Summer Olympics in Rio.

The Bronx-born Calvin Klein was the first to take mundane items like jeans and underwear and turn them into items of sexy fashion. In 1980, creating a new standard in both fashion and advertising, the 38-year-old designer hired actress Brooke Shields, then fifteen, to pose in blue jeans, asking viewers, "You want to know what comes between me and my Calvins? Nothing."

Five years after CK hit the scene, Diane Von Furstenberg, child of a Holocaust survivor, one-time wife of a prince whose mother was the heiress to the Fiat automobile fortune, introduced the fashion world to the knitted jersey "wrap dress", an example of which, due to its influence on women's fashion, is in the collection of the Costume Institute of the Metropolitan Museum of Art. She quickly grew into a global luxury lifestyle brand available in over 70 countries.

Jews have always been the backbone of the American garment industry, and their entrepreneurial talent and energies pushed them to define American style on their own terms. Starting with a promising idea and a driven, ambitious attitude, they chased a dream.

Marc Jacobs, fired by Perry Ellis in 1993 for designing a grunge look, became creative director for Louis Vuitton, and for his own line, where he has made grunge both feminine and profitable.

Zac Posen, who as a child stole yarmulkes from his grandparents' synagogue to make dresses for dolls, is still dressing dolls, winning praise from clients Natalie Portman, Rihanna, Kate Winslet, Cameron Diaz, Jennifer Lopez, and Beyoncé, for the feminine aesthetic of his design.

Warren Hirsch, President of Murjani International, created the designer label "Gloria Vanderbilt." Alfred Slaner headed Kayser-Roth, once the largest clothing manufacturer in the world. French born Maurice Bidermann was the mastermind of one of the largest clothes manufacturing networks in the world, employing 13,000 workers in 34 factories, producing Pierre Cardin and Yves St. Laurent suits. The Guess Company was founded by the Marciano brothers. The modern bra was a Jewish marketing invention, promoted by the Maiden Form Brassiere Co., owned by William and Ida Rosenthal. Hattie Carnegie led a fashion empire that set the pace for American fashion for nearly three decades. Millstein coats and suits, Puritan Fashions, Hartmarx (originally Hart, Schaffner and Marx) added to the more familiar names in the fashion industry landscape.

Israel Myers, the son of a tailor, originated the London Fog raincoat. Estelle Sommers founded the Capezio dancewear brand. Ann Klein has become a widely recognized designer company, as has Donna Karan and her DKNY label. Isaac Mizrahi created a brand that is the epitome of iconic American fashion and stands for timeless, cosmopolitan style. Tommy Hilfiger believes his brand is a living thing, that has to be nurtured "like you nurture a child," keeping it young, healthy, tech-savvy, and relevant. Rudy Gernreich was an Austrian-born American fashion designer whose avant-garde clothing designs were generally regarded as "innovative and dynamic fashion." His "monokini," consisting of only a brief, close-fitting bottom and two thin straps, was the first women's topless swimsuit. Hans Werner "John" Weitz was a successful menswear designer, selling affordable but stylish clothing that featured his image in its advertising throughout the world. Bijan was an Iranian designer of menswear and fragrances, whose exclusive boutique on Rodeo Drive in Beverly Hills has been described as "the most expensive store in the world." Among his clients, Bijan claimed to count five American Presidents - both George Bush and his son (George Bush, Jr.), Barack Obama, Ronald Reagan, and Bill Clinton, as well as politicians Tony Blair and Vladimir Putin. Designer Arnold Scassi's last name is Isaacs (his last name spelled backwards). A Canadian fashion designer, Scassi created gowns for First Ladies Mamie Eisenhower, Barbara Bush, Hillary Clinton, and Laura Bush, in addition to such notable personalities as Joan Crawford, Ivana Trump, Princess Yasmin Aga Khan, Lauren Bacall, Diahann Carroll, Elizabeth Taylor, Catherine Deneuve, Brooke Astor, Arlene Francis, and Mary Tyler Moore. Kenneth Cole is an American fashion house with an international brand operating retail and outlet stores, catalogs, and websites worldwide. He uses fashion as a medium to promote socially conscious ads to help fight various causes, from AIDS to homelessness. Liz Claiborne founded her company with her Jewish husband Arthur Ortenberg, and became the first woman to become chair and CEO of a Fortune 500 company.

The head of the French luxury jewelry firm, Cartier, (Alain Perrin) is Jewish. Kenneth Jay Lane's "Jewish jewels," have been worn by Jacqueline Onassis and Audrey Hepburn. The president and CEO of Christian Dior is Jewish. The Chanel company, was founded by Coco Chanel (the lady was not Jewish), but built to power by the Wertheimer brothers. In 1924, Chanel sold 90% of the rights to Chanel No. 5 to Pierre Wertheimer, who with his brother Paul, owned Bourjois, the largest cosmetics company in France. They bought out Chanel, couture house, perfume, and all, in 1954.

L'Oreal, the cosmetics giant, was founded by the Bettencourt family. Diane Von Furstenberg (original name Diane Simone Michelle Halfin) founded a fragrance and fashion empire. Samuel Rubin founded the Faberge perfume company. Max Factor built a cosmetics empire. The names of Helena Rubenstein and Estee Lauder (born Josephine Esther Menzer) became virtual synonyms for cosmetics in the 20th century. Adrien Arpel opened 500 skin care salons across America. Vidal Sassoon built an empire based on hair care. Jack Rosen is chairman of the Hazel Bishop cosmetics company. The Gottlieb family founded the Gottex swimwear line. Chicago's Irving Harris became a millionaire with his Toni Home Permanent. And then there's Mr. Blackwell, a Jewish fashion designer, who created the popular "world's 'best' and 'worst' dressed lists."

Sidney Kimmel heads the Jones Apparel Group; its clothing lines include Jones New York, Evan-Picone, Sayville, and Nine West shoe stores. The CEO of the Jo Ann Stores chain (1065 stores nationwide), a/k/a Jo Ann Fabrics is Alan Rossman, whose father co-founded the firm. The founders of the Banana Republic clothing retail chain were Bill Rosenzweig, and Mel and Patricia Ziegler. The Eddie Bauer outdoor clothing empire is headed of course by Eddie Bauer (yes, Eddie's Jewish). Jeffrey Swartz is the president and CEO of the Timberland shoe and boot firm. Howard Gross is the CEO of Miller's Outpost chain of 220 stores. Robert Siegel is the CEO of the Stride Rite store chain. Donald Fisher is founder and CEO of the giant clothes retailer, The Gap. The CEO of The Limited, Inc. is Leslie Wexner. The Limited's 3000 outlets and brands include Abercrombie and Fitch, Structure, Express, Lane Bryant, Henri Bendel,

Bath & Body Works, and Victoria's Secret, among others. Linda Wachner, president of Max Factor, U.S. Division, maneuvered a takeover of the Warnaco Group, effectively seizing control of much of the women's underwear market (including the brand names Warners, Olga, Valentino, Scaagi, Ungaro, Bob Mackie and Fruit of the Loom). Wachner was henceforth the CEO of Warnaco, becoming one of the most powerful businesswomen in America.

H. Stern's international scope (160 stores in 12 countries), and involvement in every detail of the production of its jewels and watches is unmatched in the jewelry industry, and is often present at the most sought-after places in the world...on the wrists, necks, and fingers of Hollywood celebrities (Catherine Zeta-Jones, Angelina Jolie, Liv Tyler, Jennifer Lopez, Debra Messing, Sharon Stone, and even Britney Spears, to name a few), all style icons that have graced magazine covers and have made those famous "red carpet appearances."

And finally, New York's Fashion Institute of Technology grew from the dream of a small group of successful Eastern European Jewish immigrant manufacturers, who ultimately created a thriving college of art and design, business and technology. It is now ranked among the top five fashion schools in the world.
Amazing what two cents will get you.

A.S. Winston

"WHAT SOAP IS TO THE BODY, LAUGHTER IS TO THE SOUL"

Handed down since Moses was kvetching about having to cross the desert in his bare feet, Jewish humor emanated from Eastern Europe where the Hebrews overcame some seriously hellacious circumstances on the way to the Promised Land. "Laughter through tears," they called it.

Over the years it came in the form of slapstick (The Three Stooges), physical comedy (Jerry Lewis), smart-aleck observation (Norman Lear), occasional cruelty (Rodney Dangerfield), uncontrolled neurosis (Shelley Berman) and bemused irreverence (Jerry Seinfeld).

The religious theology itself also contributed to the craft, encouraging believers to question authority, even God (Lenny Bruce), and test audiences to the max (Don Rickles).

In the early twentieth century, Jews used stand-up comedy to get out of tough, poor neighborhoods and their overbearing mothers' living rooms. Kids with wicked senses of humor got on stage in vaudeville, at burlesque halls, Yiddish variety houses and the numerous resorts in the Catskills.

The Borscht Belt arose out of the tradition of Yiddish theater, in Jewish resort areas in the Catskill Mountains of New York. Many of the most famous Jewish comedians of the twentieth century launched their careers there. Later, they gained a wider mainstream audience with the rise of vaudeville. Common themes among American Jewish comedians included their heritage as Jews, their experience of living between two worlds (ethnic and mainstream), their anxiety of living as a minority in America, and their personal imperfections of American culture.

Q: Why don't Jewish mothers drink?
A: Alcohol interferes with their suffering.

The relationship between Jews and comedy has been noted frequently by scholars, serious talk-show hosts, psychologists, and everybody who thinks it's important to discuss this phenomenon. No one can ignore the powerful Jewish presence in American comedy.

In America, Jews are a white minority. Think about that: we can live comfortably, practice freely and bowl adequately. But being a Jew in America is like using left-handed scissors. You can make it work, but it doesn't always "feel right." After being an oppressed minority more or less continuously for more than five thousand years, you either get a sense of humor about it, or commit suicide.

Sometime shortly after birth, an American Jew realizes he's in the minority. That realization takes a little longer if the delivering obstetrician is Jewish, or if the baby's born in New York City. It's not heartbreaking, it's not debilitating and it's clearly not as difficult as being a nonwhite minority. Judaism is something of a burden though. And that accounts the need for humor as much as anything else.

Jews go by many names: "Children of Israel," "Members of the Tribe," "Executive Producer." But perhaps the most descriptive is "Chosen People." Chosen. Set apart by God. The world is incomplete, and God chose the Jews to complete it (Oy!!!). This concept is embodied in the Hebrew phrase "tikkun olam," which roughly translates to "putting the world in order," and conveys an obligation on Jews to pursue social justice. And even though countless Jews have never heard this phrase, we all carry it in our hearts, somehow.

But how does a Jew, even a religiously ignorant Jew, achieve these ends? How does a Jew "complete the world?" Charitable donation? Labor organization? How about a New York Times op-ed? Somewhere there is a nagging voice telling us that everything is not all right. It's hard to say if it's the voice of God, the voice of history, or the voice of our mothers. Persecuted people have two things they can do to win their point. They can punch back, or they can defuse it with laughter. Can making a joke mend the world? It couldn't hurt.

While Jews account for 2.0% of the USA's population, approximately 70% of the USA's working comedians are Jewish. As Sally famously said to Harry, "You do the math." From the Borscht Belt shtick of Mel Brooks, to the Hollywood hijinks of the Marx Brothers, Jewish humor has defined comedy in 20th century America.

A Jewish boy comes home to his mother and tells her he has met a wonderful girl, and they are to be married.

"Oh, that's nice" says Momma. "And what is this girl's name?"

The son tells her that his bride-to-be is a Native American and is called Morning Mist.

"That's nice, honey" says Momma, trying to keep a straight face.

The son then tells his Momma that he wants to be called by his "new" Native American name too, and that from now on she should call him "Running Deer".

"OK, honey, whatever you wish" says Momma.

Then the son says, "You should get a Native American name too, Momma".

"I've already got one," replies Momma. "It's Sitting Shiva."

Jacob died. His will provided sixty thousand dollars for an elaborate funeral. As the last guests departed her home, his wife Sarah, turned to her oldest and dearest friend Rachel, "Well, I'm sure Jacob would be pleased," she said.

"I'm sure you're right," replied Rachel, who then lowered her voice and leaned in close. "How much did this really cost?"

Sarah said, "All of it? Sixty thousand."

"No," Rachel exclaimed. "I mean it was very nice, but sixty thousand dollars?"

"The funeral was eight thousand dollars," Sarah replied. "I donated five hundred dollars to the synagogue. The miscellaneous expenses were another five hundred dollars. The rest went for the memorial stone."

Rachel computed quickly. "Fifty-one thousand dollars for a memorial stone? My God, how big is it?"

"Six and a half carats."

Q: What is the technical term for a divorced Jewish woman?

A: "Plaintiff."

Q: How does a Jewish wife cheat on her husband?
A: She has a headache with the mailman.

Q: What is a Jewish woman's perfect breakfast?
A: She's sitting at the table with her gourmet coffee.
Her son's picture is on the box of Wheaties.
Her daughter's picture is on the cover of Fortune.
Her boyfriend is on the cover of GQ
And her husband is on the back of the milk carton.

David had a terrible accident. His manhood was mangled and torn from his body. The doctor reassured him that modern medicine made it possible for his manhood to be rebuilt, but insurance didn't cover the expense. It was considered cosmetic. He had three choices – 'average' for $8,500; 'a lot better than average' for $12,500; and 'When the saints come marching in,' for $25,000.

David was sure he'd want, at the very least, 'a lot better than average.' The doctor suggested that he discuss it with his wife privately before a final decision was made. The doctor left the room and while he was gone David called his wife and told her their options. Several minutes later the doctor returned and found David looking less than enthusiastic.

"Did you make a decision?" the doctor asked.
"Yes," said David. "We're remodeling the kitchen!"

Q: What's the difference between a lady who sells her favors for money, a lady with a healthy sexual appetite, and a Jewish housewife?
A: The lady who sells her favors for money says impatiently, "Aren't you done yet?"

The lady with a healthy sexual appetite says, "So soon?"

The Jewish housewife says, "Beige, I think I'll paint the ceiling beige."

JEWISH WOMEN DON'T HAVE HOT FLASHES, THEY HAVE POWER SURGES.

Goldie accompanied her husband to the doctor's office. After his check-up, the doctor called her into his office alone. He said, "Your husband is suffering from a very severe stress disorder. If you don't do the following, your husband will surely die. Each morning, fix him a healthy breakfast. Be pleasant at all times. For lunch make him a nutritious meal. Enjoy his company. For dinner prepare an especially nice meal for him. Don't burden him with chores. Don't discuss your problems with him, as it will only make his stress worse. No nagging. And most importantly, make love with your husband several times a week. If you can do this for the next six to nine months, I think your husband will regain his health completely."

On the way home, Goldie's husband asked, "What did the doctor say?"

"You're going to die."

The Italian says, "I'm tired and thirsty. I must have wine."

The Frenchman says, "I'm tired and thirsty. I must have cognac."

The Russian says, "I'm tired and thirsty. I must have vodka."

The German says, "I'm tired and thirsty. I must have beer."

The Mexican says, "I'm tired and thirsty. I must have tequila."

The Jew says, "I'm tired and thirsty. I must have diabetes."

A Rabbi, a Priest and a Monk are talking about how they choose to give to God. The Monk says that he draws a line down the middle of the room and then throws the money into the air. Whatever lands on the left side goes to God, and whatever lands on the right goes to the Monk. The Priest says that he has a similar scheme. He draws a circle on the floor, then throws the money into the air. Whatever lands in the circle goes to God, and whatever lands outside goes to him. The Rabbi says that he too has a similar idea. He takes the money, and throws it into the air. Whatever stays in the air belongs to God.

There is a big controversy these days concerning when life begins. In Jewish tradition the fetus is not considered a viable human being until after graduation from medical school.

When an Orthodox Jew talks to God, he says, "Ribono Shel Olam" (Master of the World). When a Conservative Jew is in touch with God, he says "Avinu Malkeinu" (Our Father, Our King). A Reform Jew addresses God as "Oh Lord, Thou Art One." A Reconstructionist says, "To whom it may concern."

Today's Short Reading from the Bible... from Genesis: "And God promised man that good and obedient wives would be found in all corners of the earth." Then He made the earth round...and He laughed and laughed and laughed!

A Park Avenue society girl arrived in Miami Beach on a day in which the temperature had zoomed to well over 100. As she got out of her car, she was overcome by the heat and fainted. A crowd of concerned bystanders gathered around her.
"Get a glass of water!" shouted one.
"Get a doctor!" screamed another.
"Open up the mink!" yelled the third.

The following was overheard at a recent fundraising party.
"My ancestry goes back all the way to Alexander the Great," said Christine, who then turned to Miriam and asked, "And how far back does your family go?"
"I don't know," replied Miriam, "All of our records were lost in the flood."

Q. Why is a Jewish divorce so expensive?
A. Because it's worth it!

Q: What is Jewish birth control after 50?
A: Nudity.

Q: What happened when Naomi inserted an ad in the classifieds that read, "Husband wanted, must be Jewish."
A: The next day she received 200 letters all saying the exact same thing. "TAKE MINE!"

Q: What's the worst thing a Jewish woman can get on her 25th anniversary?
A: Morning sickness.

Q: What makes a Jewish woman lose all sexual desire?
A: Wedding cake.

Q: What's the most effective way to remember a Jewish wife's birthday?
A: Forget it once.

Q: What is the definition of the Israeli Jewish mother?
A: Until they die themselves, they clean, cook, and kill.

A Jewish grandma and her grandson are at the beach. He's playing in the water, she is standing on the shore not wanting to get her feet wet, when all of a sudden a huge wave appears from nowhere and crashes directly onto the spot where the boy is wading. The water recedes and the boy is no longer there, he was swept away.

The grandma holds her hands to the sky, screams and cries: "Lord, my god. How could you? Haven't I been a wonderful grandmother? Haven't I been a wonderful mother? Haven't I kept a kosher home, given to charity, lit candles every Friday night, and tried my very best to live a life that you would be proud of?"

A voice booms from the sky, "ALL RIGHT ALREADY!"

A moment later another huge wave appears out of nowhere and crashes on the beach. As the water recedes, the boy is standing there. He is smiling and splashing around as if nothing had ever happened.

The voice booms again. "I HAVE RETURNED YOUR GRANDSON. ARE YOU SATISFIED?"
She responds, "HE HAD A HAT!"

There are a number of mechanical devices which increase sexual arousal, particularly in Jewish women. Chief among these is the Mercedes Benz SLS convertible.

Q. Define mixed feelings in a Jewish household?
A. When you see your mother-in-law backing off a cliff in your new car.

Q: Under what circumstances can a Jewish husband and wife enjoy a simultaneous moment of passion?
A: When the judge signs the divorce papers.

A Jewish man is walking on the beach when he discovers a bottle containing a genie. He rubs it and the genie appears, promising to grant him one wish.
He says, "Peace in the Middle East, that's my wish."
The genie looks concerned, then says "No, I'm sorry, that's just not possible. Some things just can't be changed. Do you have another wish?"
"Okay," the man says, "I have had a question all my life, and I wonder if you could explain something to me. Would you tell me how the mind of a Jewish woman works?"
The genie pauses for another moment and then says "Define peace?"

David comes home one day to find his wife Rachel crying. "What's the matter?" asks David.

"I've just found out that you've been having an affair with your secretary. How could you do this to me? Haven't I always been a good wife to you? Haven't I cooked for you, raised your children, and always been by your side when you needed me?"

David confesses, "It's true, you really are the best wife a man could hope for. You make me happy in all ways, except one."

"What's that?" asks Rachel.

"You don't moan when we make love," replies David.

"Do you mean that if I did moan, you'd stop running around? I can moan. Let's go to bed now so I'll show you that I can moan during love making."

So they go upstairs, get undressed and get beneath the sheets.

As they kiss, Rachel asks, "Now, David, should I moan now?"

"No, not yet." David begins fondling Rachel.

"What about now? Should I moan now?"

"No, I'll tell you when."

David and Rachel begin to make love.

"Is it time for me to moan, David?"

"Wait, I'll tell you when."

Suddenly, David yells, "Now, Rachel, moan."

"YOU WOULDN'T BELIEVE WHAT A DAY I'VE JUST HAD!"

Jewish proverb: "A Jewish wife will forgive and forget, but she'll never forget what she forgave."

Three sons of a Yiddishe Mama left their homeland, went abroad and prospered. They discussed the gifts they were able to give their old mother.

Avraham, the first, said: "I built a big house for our mother."

Moishe, the second, said: "I sent her a Mercedes with a driver."

David, the youngest, said: "You remember how our mother enjoys reading the bible. Now she can't see very well. I sent her a remarkable parrot that recites the whole bible. Mama just has to name the chapter and verse."

Soon thereafter, a letter of thanks came from their mother.

"Avraham," she said, "the house you built is so huge. I live only in one room, but I have to clean the whole house. Moishe, I am too old to travel. I stay most of the time at home so I rarely use the Mercedes. And that driver has shpilkas. He's a pain in the tuchas. But David," she said, "the chicken was delicious."

Q: What's the difference between a Jewish woman with PMS and a pit bull?

A: Lipstick!

A Jewish friend of mine just got divorced. He and his ex-wife split the house. He got the outside.

*Jewish men are like a fine wine. They start out as grapes, and it's up to Jewish women to stomp the **** out of them until they turn into something acceptable to have dinner with.*

A man is lying on the operating table, about to be operated on by his son, the surgeon. The father says, "Son, think of it this way. If anything happens to me, your mother is coming to live with you."

Do you know the difference between a non-Jewish wife and a Jewish wife? The non-Jewish wife tells her husband to buy Viagra. The Jewish wife tells her husband to buy Pfizer.

Abe walks into his local CVS pharmacy and asks for some condoms.

"Yes sir, do you want the Catholic pack, the Protestant pack or the Jewish pack?"

Abe asks, "What's the difference?"

The pharmacist replies, "The Catholic pack has six, one for each day of the week, but never on Sunday. The Protestant pack has eight, one for each day of the week, and twice on Sunday. And of course the Jewish pack has twelve."

"Why twelve?" asks Abe.

The pharmacist sighs and counts on his fingers, "January, February, March...."

In a survey, 80% of Jewish women thought their ass was too fat. 15% said their ass was too thin, and the other 5% said they didn't care...they would have married him anyway.

Rabbi Rabinovitz answers his phone.
"Hello?"
"Hello, is this Rabbi Rabinovitz?"
"It is."
"This is the Internal Revenue Service. Can you help us?"
"I'll try."
"Do you know Sam Cohen?"
"I do."

"Is he a member of your congregation?"
"He is."
"Did he donate $10,000 to the synagogue rebuilding fund last year?"
"He will!"

What is the source of the Jewish sense of humor? Is it nature or nurture (perhaps a bit of both). The fact is that Judaism is big on self-examination. We make fun of our own imperfections.

It comes from realizing that we are truly nothing compared to the Almighty. Mix in a bit of cynicism (after all, Jews probably invented small print), sarcasm (you do know what that is, right?), and a healthy dose of neurosis (taken from a combination of factors, like Jewish parents and the constant challenge of balancing a physical existence with spiritual goals), and (drumroll), we have the funny Jew.

For the past century and more, American comedy has drawn its strength and soul from the comic genius of Jewish performers and writers. An incomplete listing of names makes the point: Woody Allen, Roseanne Barr, Belle Barth, Jack Benny, Gertrude Berg, Milton Berle, Shelley Berman, Sandra Bernhard, Fanny Brice, Albert Brooks, Mel Brooks, Lenny Bruce, George Burns, Sid Caesar, Billy Crystal, Rodney Dangerfield, Fran Drescher, Totie Fields, Buddy Hackett, Goldie Hawn, Judy Holliday, Madeline Kahn, Andy Kaufman, Danny Kaye, Wendy Liebman, Jerry Lewis, The Marx Brothers, Jackie Mason, Elaine May, Molly Picon, Gilda Radner, Don Rickles, Joan Rivers, Mort Sahl, Adam Sandler, Jerry Seinfeld, Sarah Silverman, Jon Stewart, Ben Stiller, The Three Stooges, Sophie Tucker, Lewis Black, Brad

Garrett, Henny Youngman, Andy Kaufman, Alan King, Red Buttons, Rita Rudner, Phil Silvers, Carl Reiner, Bette Midler, Victor Borge, Eddie Cantor, Larry David, The Ritz Brothers, Ish Kabibble, Richard Lewis, Larry Storch, Norm Crosby, Ed Wynn, Robert Klein, Oscar Levant, Steven Wright, Al Jolson, Jerry Stiller, Morey Amsterdam, David Steinberg, Marty Ingels, Rob Reiner, Harvey Korman, Jack Carter, Sam Levenson, Gene Wilder, Zero Mostel, Andrew Dice Clay, Myron Cohen, Jack E. Leonard, Bob Saget, Anne Meara, Allan Sherman, Edward Asner, George Jessel, Robert Schimmel, Marty Allen, Dick Shawn, Bert Lahr, Shecky Greene, Gary Shandling, Gabe Kaplan, Jon Lovitz, Paul Reiser, Harold Ramis, Daniel Stern, Jan Murray, Elayne Boosler, David Brenner, Sandra Bernhard, Soupy Sales, Yakov Smirnoff, Jason Alexander, Sasha Baron Cohen, Chelsea Handler….the list just goes on and on and on and on. These men and women, among many others, form the canon of Jewish-American comedy.

Q: You're at a Jewish wedding. How can you tell if it's Orthodox, Reform, or Liberal?
A: In an Orthodox wedding, the bride's mother is pregnant. In a Reform wedding, the bride is pregnant. In a Liberal wedding the Rabbi is pregnant.

Jack Benny met his wife at a Marx Brothers seder. He was a violinist for Minnie Marx, the mother of the Marx Brothers, who, at the time, were also a musical act. Every one of them was working the Borscht Belt.

Groucho Marx danced a two-minute Charleston on top of the bunker where Hitler died. One of his best friends was Alice Cooper, the rock star (yep, Jewish). The

Hollywood sign in Los Angeles was falling into disrepair, and in 1978 the local municipality auctioned it off — each celebrity could buy a letter, and Alice Cooper bought two of the 'Os' in the "Hollywood" sign in memory of Groucho. Groucho died three days after Elvis Presley, so he got very little media attention. His children found a note that said he wished to be buried above Marilyn Monroe.

Mel Brooks came up with the 2,000-year-old man because he suffered an attack of gout, and he was in such pain that he said, "I feel like a 2,000-year-old man." The name somehow stuck. Of course the point is totally absurd…. the idea that a 2,000-year-old man should be Yiddish (Yoda before his time?), but it made the world laugh.

Moe Howard (born Moses Horwitz) from the Three Stooges, was the first American actor to portray Adolf Hitler in the 1940 film short, "You Natzy Spy." In the 1941 sequel, "I'll Never Heil Again," Curly (aka Jerome Horwitz) played a field marshal who reports to Moe, a dictator, "We bombed 56 hospitals, 85 schools, 42 kindergartens, four cemeteries and other vital military objects." That was pretty powerful stuff for the Three Stooges.

A man calls his mother in Florida: "Mom, how are you?"

"Not too good," she says. "I've been very weak."

"Why are you so weak?" he asks

"Because I haven't eaten in 38 days."

"That's terrible," he says. "Why haven't you eaten in 38 days?"

"Because I didn't want my mouth should be full if you called."

And finally, ever receive one of these telegrams when waiting for the family to come visit for the holidays: *"Begin worrying. Details to follow."*

SAY IT LOUD, AND SAY IT PROUD....but definitely begin worrying.

"ROSEBUD"

If you want to understand the movie industry, you must first understand the Jews.

These European inventors of Hollywood were named Fox, Zukor, Warner, Mayer, Selznick, Lasky, Goldfish and Laemmle. William Fox was originally Fuchs Vilmos. Schmuel Gelbfisz became Sam Goldfish then Samuel Goldwyn.

For millennia, Jews conveyed their values through stories. We weren't the first to discover how effective narrative is in entertaining, teaching and ultimately shaping reality, but we did become expert at it, and raised "the Word" to the level of the sacred. Walk into any synagogue, open the doors of the ark and there lay The Story, written on the holy Torah. Enter any cinema, part the curtain, and there appears the story, filmed for the screen.

Movies are in the business of escape, and Jews are escape artists. Just look at our history. Harry Houdini was the greatest magician of all time. Movies allowed Jews to do relatively easily what it took Houdini years to perfect...to disappear as one kind of man and re-appear as another; to escape your identity. Houdini was born Erik Weisz, and in the act of escaping, helped others escape through entertainment.

Broncho Billy Anderson starred in over 500 movies, most of which he produced and directed as well. Broncho Billy was the Clooney, Downey and Pitt of his generation, except his real name was Max Aronson, and he was a failed Jewish door-to-door salesman from Little Rock, Ark.

In Hollywood, real men became ideal men, and real life became ideal life. Those two forces, the real and the ideal, are forever in conflict in the Jewish soul. Our stories and traditions present the world as it is, flawed, broken, sometimes bitter, but also as it should be, ideal, moral, sweet. Hollywood's beginnings stemmed from immigrant ideals and emotions. In Hollywood you could wipe away the past. A Goldfish could turn into a Goldwyn and an Aronson into a cowboy.

It was Jewish entertainers and entrepreneurs who discovered film in America. Their films initially served as fantasy lifestyles, an escape from the city slums into prestige and wealth, fantastic images of their values, tastes and aspirations, sympathetically portrayed. Their movies reflected their feelings. As films gained much popularity and praise, the Jewish entrepreneurs used their prominent business sense, thus creating the film factory known as Hollywood in Los Angeles, California. Jews created an industry that struggled to blend the real and the ideal. If God created man in his own image, Jews created Hollywood in theirs.

The accepted view of the Golden Age of Hollywood goes something like this: working from literate scripts, using the talents of glamorous actors and actresses (the likes of which are no longer seen), brilliant directors made films that still have the power to move, charm and amuse.

Those European inventors of Hollywood weren't after money, or power, at least not for their own sake. What they wanted was status and acceptance as Americans, which, as East European Jews, was denied to them elsewhere.

The moguls concluded that if you are going to succeed in America, you can't be Jewish or European. What they did was create their own America.

And the irony is that the America imagined by this group of enterprising immigrants, Harry Cohn, Adolph Zukor, Louis B. Mayer, the Warner brothers, became the real America. Indeed, far from stifling cinematic creativity, the moguls invented everything we mean by the word "Hollywood," and in the process, they redefined the values of a nation.

Movies are a rollercoaster ride that transcends people into a whole different world fresh out of somebody's imagination. They allow us to take a break from the burdens of work and stress, because, after we have put the kids to bed, done the dishes, cleaned the house, and finished our taxes, we can finally relax, sit down and watch an entertaining movie.

At the movie high tide in 1946 (before television invaded us), 80 million people a week went to the movies. It was America's community habit.

The reason movies are so ardently revered is because it lets us escape into a world which is far from the daily realities of our lives. For more than a century, movies have impacted our lives, and will continue to impact those of future generations.

Hollywood was created primarily by a remarkable group of men who fit into an incredible small demographic: European Jewish immigrants, most of them poor, most of them from Manhattan's lower East Side. Together they moved across an entire nation and created the most successful form of popular entertainment in America, presenting an idealized version of American life.

Adolph Zukor was instrumental in creating Paramount; Carl Laemmle founded Universal; William Fox founded Fox Pictures, which later merged with Twentieth Century (20th Century Fox); Louis B. Mayer built MGM into Hollywood's largest studio; Harry and Jack Warner founded Warner Brothers; and the belligerent Harry Cohn was the driving force of Columbia Pictures.

One of the most striking facts is how completely these men suppressed their Jewish backgrounds in their films. Although *The Jazz Singer* is the story of a Jewish son rejecting the culture of his cantor father, the vast majority of movies produced by Hollywood in the twenties, thirties, and forties contained no identifiably Jewish characters. While an astonishing number of the people producing the movies were Jewish, it was as if they felt compelled to completely erase their backgrounds from their idealization of American life. They were trying to become a part of a nation that largely rejected them.

As "outsiders," they nonetheless excelled at creating a vision of America that incorporated many of its most cherished principles and desires. They had a vision of America that stood far removed from the reality of their own lives. Thus was born "The Golden Age Of Hollywood."

For Louis B. Mayer, Andy Hardy's America was the real America, an America where there were strong nuclear families headed by strong fathers, doting neo-Victorian mothers, and obedient, respectful children.

What united these movie moguls in deep spiritual kinship was their utter and absolute rejection of their pasts and their equally absolute devotion to their new country. For most of these men, what they provided was not America as it existed, but the America they wanted to be a part of. Something drove them to a ferocious, almost pathological, embrace of their new home, and to deny whatever they had been before settling here. These Jewish leaders "colonized" the American imagination. Their films embodied American values, the irony being they were made by people alienated from that very culture. The Jews reinvented America in the image of their fiction.

We did not invent the movies. That distinction goes to the genius of Thomas Edison. What was remarkable about the Jewish immigrants from Europe was that they organized and founded these movie studios and that it was their ability to recognize the new medium when it first came into use, shortly after their arrival in this country. It was they who made the motion picture big business.

They understood the need for making movies as reflections of American culture. They invented talking movies, technicolor, and the movie musical. From 1920 until 1960, the movie industry was at its height. From romances to crime stories and the inevitable westerns, these Jewish studio heads produced everything imaginable. An incomplete list would include…

Going My Way, Sunset Blvd., Duck Soup, The Court Jester, White Christmas, The Greatest Show On Earth, The Ten Commandments, It's A Wonderful Life, King Kong, Bringing Up Baby, Notorious, Citizen Kane, Boys Town, The Philadelphia Story, Mrs. Miniver, Father Of The Bride, The Wizard Of Oz, Easter Parade, Show Boat, An American In Paris, Singing In The Rain, Seven Brides For Seven Brothers, Gigi, Gone With The Wind, Tarzan, The Thin Man, The Andy Hardy movies, The Jazz Singer, The Adventures of Robin Hood, Casablanca, Yankee Doodle Dandy, I Am A Fugitive From A Chain Gang, \The Maltese Falcon, The Big Sleep, The Life Of Emile Zola, The Treasure Of Sierra Madre, 42nd Street, A Streetcar Named Desire, Rebel Without A Cause, A Star Is Born, Frankenstein, Cleopatra, The Grapes Of Wrath, State Fair, Miracle On 34th Street, All About Eve, Mr. Smith Goes To Washington, High Noon, Snow White And The Seven Dwarfs, The Best Years Of Our Lives, Shane, It Happened One Night, The Gold Rush, Sullivan's Travels, A Night At The Opera, Ben Hur. The African Queen, Modern Times, The Birth of a Nation, All Quiet On the Western Front, The Third Man, Fantasia, Stagecoach, Wuthering Heights, Giant, Mutiny On the Bounty, A Place in the Sun, Tom Sawyer, The Great Zeigfeld, My Man Godfrey, Topper, Lost Horizon, Goodbye Mr. Chips, The Hunchback of Notre Dame, Holiday Inn, Arsenic and Old Lace, The Bells of St. Mary's. Song of the South, The Ghost and Mrs. Muir, The Bishop's Wife, The Farmer's Daughter, The Three Musketeers, All the King's Men, King Solomon's Mines, Cinderella, Born Yesterday, Alice in Wonderland, Hans Christian Anderson, From Here to Eternity, Roman Holiday, Gentlemen Prefer Blondes, Peter Pan, Rear

Window, The Caine Mutiny, 20,000 Leagues Under the Sea, On the Waterfront, Sabrina, Mr. Roberts, Around the World in 80 Days, The King and I, High Society, Moby Dick, The Bridge on the River Kwai, Old Yeller, An Affair to Remember, Some Like it Hot.

Their imagination, however, never included Jewish themes (note the above list of movies), nor were they willing, during the Second World War, to so much as mention the persecution of their own families left behind in Eastern Europe. It is to the eternal shame of these powerful men that they sympathized with everyone from Native Americans to the aborigines of Australia, but never their fellow Jews.

The studio bosses weren't the only Jews in the movie business. There were (and still are) innumerable Jewish producers and directors, many of whom changed their names in order to escape recognition as Jews. This was also true of the numerous Jewish movie actors. If you've ever seen a movie with Kirk Douglas, you would have really watched a performance by (remember the earlier list) Issur Danielovitch Demsky. Winona Ryder was born Laura Horowitz, and the comedian Red Buttons was called Aaron Chwatt. There is even an Albert Einstein in the acting profession. He is known as Albert Brooks. Sylvia Sidney was Sophia Jasnow in her first incarnation, and Betty Perske, the cousin of the former Israeli Prime Minister Shimon Peres, became Lauren Bacall.

And then there was Broncho Billy. There may never have been a Roy Rogers or a Gene Autry had it not been for the grandson of a rabbi, who became America's first cowboy hero. Born Max Aronson in Little Rock, Arkansas, he would one day star in hundreds of westerns.

Max Aronson appeared in the. innovative film *The Great Train Robbery* (1903), then, from 1907 to 1919, he was cowpoke "Broncho Billy." Aronson, actor, writer, director, and producer of these short films, fashioned new camera techniques that fathered the Western, and co-founded the Essanay Film Manufacturing Co., which launched the careers of Gloria Swanson and Charlie Chaplin. He was honored with an Academy Award in 1958.

Yes, there are a lot of Jews in positions of influence in Hollywood, in network television, in sports, entertainment, and in many other areas of American public life. There are also a large number of Jews in medicine, law, academia, and finance. They certainly do not conspire to exercise any sort of "Jewish control" over the areas in which they work. Personally, I praise these individuals, who, through hard work and talent, have earned their place in so many areas of American life. Immigrants seeking a better life. Immigrants who picked up on the dreams and aspirations of other immigrants. Immigrants who wanted to be regarded as Americans, and then as Jews. Immigrants with two cents in their pocket and a vision for their future. I always believed that was the American dream.

The two greatest Jewish inventions of the 20th century were Hollywood and Israel. Both provided a means of refuge from the real world. Israel was founded to help Jews escape the world. Hollywood was founded to help the world escape reality.

The United States has been very good to the Jewish people, and in turn, we have contributed far more than our share to the wealth, culture, identity, individuality, and dynamic of our country.

THAT'S A WRAP!
SAY IT LOUD, AND SAY IT PROUD!

A.S. Winston

IT ALL STARTED WITH A SKIN FLICK

In 1933, a beautiful, young Austrian woman took off her clothes for a movie director. She ran through the woods, naked. She swam in a lake, naked. Pushing well beyond the social norms of the period, the movie also featured the physical and emotional peak of sexual excitation.

The most popular movie in 1933 was King Kong. But everyone in Hollywood was talking about that scandalous movie with the gorgeous, young Austrian woman.

Louis B. Mayer said she was the most beautiful woman in the world. The film was banned practically everywhere, which of course made it even more popular. The star of the film, titled *Ecstasy* was Hedwig Kiesler. She said the secret of her beauty was "to stand there and look stupid." In reality, Kiesler was anything but stupid. She was a genius. She'd grown up as the only child of a prominent Jewish banker. She was a math prodigy. She excelled at science. As she grew older, she became ruthless, using all the power her body and mind gave her.

Between the sexual roles she played in her films, her tremendous beauty, and the power of her intellect, Kiesler would confound the men in her life.

"Men are most virile and most attractive between the ages of 35 and 55. Under 35 a man has too much to learn, and I don't have time to teach him."

Her beauty made her rich for a time. She is said to have made, and spent, $30 million in her life. But her greatest accomplishment resulted from her intellect, and her invention continues to shape the world we live in today.

You see, this young Austrian starlet would take one of the most valuable technologies ever developed right from under Hitler's nose. After fleeing to America, she not only became a major Hollywood star, her name sits on one of the most important patents ever granted by the U.S. Patent Office.

At the time she made *Ecstasy*, Kiesler was married to Friedrich Mandl, Austria's leading arms maker. Mandl used his beautiful young wife as a showpiece at important business dinners with representatives of the Austrian, Italian, and German fascist forces. One of Mandl's favorite topics at these gatherings, which included meals with Hitler and Mussolini, was the technology surrounding radio-controlled missiles and torpedoes. Wireless weapons offered far greater ranges than the wire-controlled alternatives that prevailed at the time.

Hedwig Kiesler sat through these dinners "looking stupid," while absorbing everything she heard.

As a Jew, she hated Germany, and the Nazi regime. She abhorred her husband's business ambitions. Mandl responded to his willful wife by imprisoning her in his castle, Schloss Schwarzenau. In 1937, she escaped her imprisonment, drugging her maid, sneaking out of the castle wearing the maid's clothes, and ultimately selling her jewelry to finance a trip to London. She had gotten out just in time. In 1938, Germany annexed Austria.

In London, she signed a long-term contract with Louis B. Mayer, quickly becoming one of MGM's biggest stars.

But she cared far more about fighting Nazis than about making movies. At the height of her fame, in 1942, she developed a new kind of communications system, optimized for sending coded messages that couldn't be "jammed." She was building a system to kill the world's "cancer," allowing torpedoes and guided bombs to always reach their targets.

On August 11, 1942, U.S. Patent No. 2,292,387 was granted to "Hedy Kiesler Markey," which was Kiesler's married name at the time.

Most of you won't recognize the name Kiesler, nor remember the name Hedy Markey. But it's a fair bet than anyone reading this (of a certain age) will remember one of the great beauties of Hollywood's golden age, Hedy Lamarr, the name Louis B. Mayer gave to his prize actress. And the name his movie company made famous.

But not many people know that Hedwig Kiesler, a/k/a Hedy Lamarr, was one of the great pioneers of wireless communications. Her technology was developed by the U.S. Navy, which has used it ever since.

Her patent sits at the foundation of "spread spectrum technology," which we use every day when we log on to a wi-fi network or make calls with our Bluetooth-enabled phone. It lies at the heart of the massive investments being made right now in so-called fourth-generation long term evolution, more commonly referred to as "LTE" wireless technology. Today, when you use your cell phone, or experience super-fast wireless Internet access, you'll be using an extension of the technology a twenty year-old actress first conceived while sitting at dinner with Adolph Hitler.

LIFE IN A JAR

When Hitler and his Nazis built the Warsaw Ghetto and herded 500,000 Polish Jews behind its walls to await liquidation, Irena Sendler defied the Nazi machine and saved 2,500 Jewish children by smuggling them out of the ghetto.

Irena Sendler, a Senior Administrator in the Warsaw Social Welfare Department, was so appalled by the conditions in the Ghetto that she joined Zegota, the Council for Aid to Jews, organized by the Polish underground resistance movement.

To be able to enter the Ghetto legally, Irena managed to be issued a pass from Warsaw's Epidemic Control Department. She visited the Ghetto daily, reestablishing contacts, bringing food, medicines and clothing. But 5,000 people were dying every month from starvation and disease in the Ghetto, and she decided to help the Jewish children get out.

Persuading parents to part with their children was in itself a horrendous task. Finding families willing to shelter the children, and thereby willing to risk their life if the Nazis ever found out, was also not easy.

She recruited at least one person from each of the ten centers of Warsaw's Social Welfare Department. With their help, she issued hundreds of false documents with forged signatures, and successfully smuggled almost

2,500 Jewish children to safety and gave them temporary new identities.

Some children were taken out in gunnysacks or body bags. Some were buried inside loads of goods. A mechanic took a baby out in his toolbox. Some kids were carried out in potato sacks, others were placed in coffins. "Can you guarantee they will live?" Irena later recalled the distraught parents asking. She could only guarantee they would die if they stayed.

The children were given false identities and placed in homes, orphanages and convents. Sendler carefully noted, in coded form, the children's original names and their new identities. She kept the only record of their true identities in jars buried beneath an apple tree in a neighbor's back yard, across the street from German barracks, hoping she could someday dig up the jars, locate the children, and inform them of their past.

When the Nazis became aware of Irena's activities, she was arrested, imprisoned and tortured by the Gestapo. Though she was the only one who knew the names and addresses of the families sheltering the Jewish children, she withstood the torture, refusing to betray either her associates or any of the Jewish children in hiding.

Sentenced to death, Irena was saved at the last minute when Zegota members bribed one of the Germans to halt the execution. She escaped from prison but for the rest of the war she was pursued by the Gestapo.

After the war she dug up the jars and used the notes to track down the 2,500 children she placed with adoptive families and to reunite them with relatives scattered across Europe. But most lost their families during the Holocaust in Nazi death camps.

Irena Sendler did not think of herself as a hero. She claimed no credit for her actions.

In 1965 she was accorded the title Righteous among the Nations by the Yad Vashem organization in Jerusalem, and in 1991 was made an honorary citizen of Israel.

She was also awarded Poland's highest distinction, the Order of White Eagle in Warsaw in 2003.

This lovely, courageous woman was one of the most dedicated and active workers in aiding Jews during the Nazi occupation of Poland. Her courage enabled not only the survival of 2,500 Jewish children, but also generations of their descendants.

Irena Sendler passed away on May 12, 2008, at the age of 98.

A.S. Winston

ONCE UPON A TIME....A REAL LIFE FAIRY TALE

Pierre didn't know where it came from, he only knew that it came and it helped in oh-so-many ways. The money always arrived with a small short note that simply said, "Keep up the great cause, we will prevail," and was simply signed, "Manny." Pierre didn't know who Manny was. Nobody did! Not then anyway. We do now. But this was during World War II when the Black Horror was sweeping Europe. That's what Manny called it, The Black Horror, and of course he was referring to the Nazi plague that was taking over most of the continent. Pierre was a leader of the French Resistance. He fought with groups of French citizens in the best way he could, by living within main society and leading bands of armed resistance against the Germans in clandestine activities. They would ambush German patrols, blow up German installations and sabotage Nazi operations in any way they could.

The Allies were good at providing arms and weapons, but the underground also needed money. That was a commodity that was very hard to come by during the war, especially when your country is completely occupied by an invading military force. And that's where Manny came in. He sent money, and he sent a lot of it. Manny was born a Romanian Jew, who was now living in America. Manny had done very well in his life and he knew only too well what kinds of horrors were going on in his native Romania and the rest of Europe. Jews and others were being gassed and killed by the millions and he had to do something. One thing he could do was use his good fortune to help the war effort.

He had tried to join the Armed Forces, but he didn't qualify, so he did what he could. He sent money to where it was needed the most - to the resistance. As I said, Pierre was one of the leaders of the resistance. There were many, but Pierre controlled the action around the area of Normandy. He and his people were very instrumental in assisting the Allied invasion on D-Day by sabotaging and redirecting many Nazi forces moments before the actual invasion.

Much of this was possible because of the money that arrived every month. Month after month for two years money arrived for Pierre and his cause from Manny. Pierre never knew who Manny was, only that he sent money for food, clothes, gasoline and many other important things.

But years later, we learned who Manny was, that silent guardian angel of the French underground. He was one of the biggest stars in Hollywood, and a fine gentleman. It's a little known fact that a very important part of the success of the French underground came from a source they never knew: Emmanuel Goldenberg, or as you knew him, the very fine actor Edward G. Robinson.

A SECOND-RATE BASEBALL PLAYER BUT A FIRST RATE SPY.

When baseball greats Babe Ruth and Lou Gehrig went on tour in baseball-crazy Japan in 1934, some fans wondered why a third-string catcher named Moe Berg was included.

The answer was simple: Berg was a U.S. spy, speaking fifteen languages including Japanese. Moe Berg had two loves: baseball and spying.

In Tokyo, garbed in a kimono, Berg took flowers to the daughter of an American diplomat being treated in St. Luke's Hospital, the tallest building in the Japanese capital. He never delivered the flowers. The ball-player ascended to the hospital roof and filmed key features, including the harbor, military installations, and railway yards.

Eight years later, General Jimmy Doolittle studied Berg's films in planning his spectacular raid on Tokyo.

Berg's father, Bernard Berg, a pharmacist in Newark, New Jersey, taught his son Hebrew and Yiddish. In Barringer High School, Moe learned Latin, Greek and French. He graduated magna cum laude from Princeton, having added Spanish, Italian, German and Sanskrit to his linguistic quiver. During further studies at the Sorbonne in Paris, and Columbia Law School, he picked up Japanese, Chinese, Korean, Indian, Arabic, Portuguese and Hungarian, fifteen languages in all, plus some regional dialects.

While playing baseball for Princeton University, Moe Berg would often describe plays in Latin or Sanskrit. During World War II, he was parachuted into Yugoslavia to assess the value to the war effort of the two groups of partisans there. He reported back that Marshall Tito's forces were widely supported by the people. Winston Churchill ordered all-out support for the Yugoslav underground fighter, rather than Mihajlovic's Serbians. The parachute jump at age 41 undoubtedly was a challenge. But there was more to come in that same year. Berg penetrated German-held Norway, met with members of the underground and located a secret heavy water plant, part of Hitler's effort to build an atomic bomb. His information guided the Royal Air Force in a bombing raid to destroy the plant.

There still remained the question of how far had the Germans progressed in the race to build the first atomic bomb. If the Nazis were successful, they would win the war.

Berg (under the code name "Remus") was sent to Switzerland to hear leading German physicist Werner Heisenberg, a Nobel Laureate, lecture, and determine if the Nazis were close to building an A-bomb. Moe managed to slip past the SS guards at the auditorium, posing as a Swiss graduate student. The spy carried in his pocket a pistol and a cyanide pill. If the German indicated the Nazis were close to building a weapon, Berg was to shoot him, and then swallow the cyanide pill. Moe, sitting in the front row, determined that the Germans were nowhere near their goal, so he complimented Heisenberg on his speech and walked him back to his hotel.

Moe Berg's report was distributed to Britain's Prime Minister, Winston Churchill, President Franklin D. Roosevelt, and key figures in the team developing the atomic bomb.

Roosevelt responded: "Give my regards to the catcher."

Most of Germany's leading physicists had been Jewish, and had fled the Nazis mainly to Britain and the United States,

After the war, Moe Berg was awarded the Medal of Merit, America's highest honor for a civilian in wartime. But Berg refused to accept the award, as he couldn't tell people about his exploits. After his death, his sister accepted the Medal and it hangs today in the Baseball Hall of Fame, in Cooperstown, New York.

THE PEOPLE OF THE BOOK

Jewish writers from all over the globe have contributed fiction in a number of different languages, helping to document the Jewish experience, often better than most history books. The written word has saved lives, circulated powerful ideas, preserved traditions and memories, and so much more. The breathtaking scope and infectious enthusiasm of these book are a tribute to our ideals, hopes, and dreams. Indeed, literature has touched the lives of generations, and sometimes changed the course of history. Great literature transports us to a different world, a different state of mind, a different way of relating to everyday life. It stimulates our imagination.

The Jewish literary canon contains a vast mix of novels, from beloved children's stories to Pulitzer Prize winners. It includes tales of humor and tragedy, magic and love, and spans historical fiction, contemporary fiction, magical realism, and futuristic settings. Reading through this diverse list, we gain a greater understanding of a community that, while comparatively small, is incredibly diverse.

The criteria for this list was any work that could be considered "Jewish fiction," having been written by a Jewish author or dealing heavily with Jewish topics and themes, and all written in the last 100 years. While this list tilts heavily towards the circumcised brotherhood, gender inequality is non-existent when it comes to great writing. And for many of these authors, their output was much greater than a single novel.

How many of these do you recognize?

"The Diary of a Young Girl"
Anne Frank

"Catch 22"
Joseph Heller

"The Chosen,"
"My Name is Asher Lev"
Chaim Potok

"Where the Wild Things Are"
Maurice Sendak

"Death of a Salesman"
Arthur Miller

"Where the Sidewalk Ends"
Shel Silverstein

"Portnoy's Complaint"
"Goodbye, Columbus"
Philp Roth

"Exodus"
Leon Uris

"Herzog"
Saul Bellow

"The Collected Stories of Isaac Bashevis Singer"
Isaac Bashevis Singer

"Friday the Rabbi Slept Late"
Harry Kemmelman

"Rosenkranz and Guildenstern are Dead"
Tom Stoppard

"The Princess Bride"
William Goldman

"The Natural"
Bernard Malamud

"The Apprenticeship of Duddy Kravitz"
Mordecai Richler

"I, Robot"
Isaac Asimov

"The Winds of War"
Herman Wouk

"The Children's Hour"
Lillian Hellman

"Sophie's Choice"
William Styron

"When Harry Met Sally"
Nora Ephron

"Amadeus"
Peter Shaffer

"SeinLanguage"
Jerry Seinfeld

"The Joys of Yiddush"
Leo Rosten

"Tuesdays with Morrie"
Mitch Albom

"The Guns of August"
Barbara Tuchman

"The Executioner's Song"
Norman Mailer

"A Thousand Clowns"
Herb Gardner

"Side Effects"
Woody Allen

"Chutzpah"
Alan M. Dershowitz

"Tropic of Capricorn"
Henry Miller

"The Metamorphosis"
Franz Kafka

"In Search of Lost Time"
Marcel Proust

"The Catcher in the Rye"
J.D. Salinger

"A Contract with God"
Will Eisner

"Are You There God? It's Me, Margaret"
Judy Blume

"The Odessa Tales"
Isaac Babel

"The Pawnbroker"
Edward Lewis Wallant

"The Trial of God"
Elie Wiesel

"Bech, a Book"
John Updike

"What Makes Sammy Run?"
Budd Schulberg

"The New Colossus"
Emma Lazarus

Of course there are other Jewish writers of note whose works may not be considered "Jewish fiction," but are known universally.

Oscar Hammerstein II, whose works for the American theater included "Show Boat," "Oklahoma!" "Carousel," "South Pacific," "The King and I," and "The Sound of Music." Ayn Rand wrote "The Fountainhead," and "Atlas Shrugged." Edna Ferber wrote "So Big," "Show Boat," "Giant," "Ice Palace," "Saratoga Trunk," and "Cimarron." Herman Wouk wrote "The Caine Mutiny." Mackinley Kantor wrote "Andersonville." Saul Bellow wrote "Humboldt's Gift." Carrie Fisher wrote "Postcards from the Edge." Carl Sagan wrote "Contact," and the "Cosmos" series for PBS television. Stan Lee wrote, or co-wrote "Spider-Man," "the Hulk," "Iron Man," "Thor," and "the X-Men." Sidney Sheldon wrote "The Other Side of Midnight," and "Rage of Angels." Carl Bernstein wrote "All the President's Men." Boris Pasternak wrote "Dr. Zhivago." E. L. Doctorow wrote "Ragtime," and "Billy Bathgate." Arthur Koestler wrote "Darkness at Noon." And Broadway playwright Neil Simon, wrote "Come Blow your Horn," "Barefoot in the Park," "The Odd Couple," "Lost in Yonkers," "Plaza Suite," "The Sunshine Boys," "The Prisoner of Second Avenue," "Sweet Charity," "California Suite," "Chapter Two," "Brighton Beach Memoirs," and "Biloxi Blues."

Some other names you might be familiar with are Sholom Aleichem, Sigmund Freud, Gertrude Stein, Faye Kellerman, Jonathon Kellerman, Albert Einstein, Maimonides, Nathaniel West, Irwin Shaw, Robert Bloch, Michael Chabon, Harlan Ellison, Jules Pfeiffer, Laura Z. Hobson, Fannie Hurst, Rona Jaffe, Erica Jong, Roger Kahn, Ira Levin, Sara Peretsky, Dorothy Parker, S.J.

Perelman, Harold Robbins, Judith Rossner, Irving Shulman, Joel Siegel, Susan Sontag, Daniel Stern, Calvin Trillin, Scott Turow, Judith Viorst, Nathaniel West, Paddy Chayefsky, Clifford Odets, Rod Serling, Aaron Sorkin, Wendy Wasserstein, George S. Kaufman, Moss Hart, Carl Reiner, and Art Buchwald.

The written word is the basic building block of knowledge. It allows us a way to leave information behind, to be read years, decades, centuries later. It is the power of the written word that has saved lives, circulated powerful ideas, preserved traditions, conserved memories, safeguarded history, and so much more. Yes, we really have held up our end of the "People of the Book."

SAY IY LOUD, AND SAY IT PROUD!

BUT THEY LOVED THEIR MOTHERS...

Organized crime emerged within the American Jewish community during the late 19th and early 20th centuries. It has been referred to variously in media and popular culture as the Jewish Mob, Jewish Mafia, Kosher Mafia, and Kosher Nostra. Their roots lay in the ethnic neighborhoods of the Lower East Side in New York, Brownsville in Brooklyn, Maxwell Street in Chicago, and Boyle Heights in Los Angeles.

Like other newly arrived groups in American history, a few Jews who considered themselves "blocked" from respectable professions, used crime as a means to "make good" economically. The market for vice flourished during Prohibition, and Jews joined with others to exploit the artificial market created by the legal bans on alcohol, gambling, paid sex, and narcotics. It was the period between the World Wars, the eras of Prohibition and the Great Depression that saw the rise of the American Jewish gangster as a force.

In 1919, the United States government attempted to regulate morality by outlawing the manufacture and sale of alcoholic beverages. Prohibition offered an enormous opportunity for those with the chutzpah to provide what society still wanted, namely "booze."

Another contributing factor to the rise of the "kosher nostra," was the morality of the age. At all levels of society, this was a time when "anything goes," and when flaunting the rules was the norm.

It was in this milieu that the Jewish gangster rose to prominence. Contrary to modern Jewish criminals (yes, we have those today, too) who are involved mostly in white-collar crime such as fraud, insider-trading, or embezzlement, these men engaged in extortion, gambling, narcotics peddling, boot-legging, and murder. For a time they dominated the rackets in Boston, Cleveland, Detroit, Newark, Philadelphia, and New York.

A composite portrait of the "typical" Jewish gangster of this period would show him to be a second generation American male of Eastern European parentage, city bred, and in his early twenties. His parents would be working class and traditional. He would not have finished high school and would remain strongly attached to his family throughout his life.

He chose crime because it was the quickest way for him to achieve material success, power, recognition, and status. It was a means to become a "somebody," moving up and out of their neighborhood ghetto. Legitimate work was hard, dull, and offered only slow economic and social mobility. Crime was exciting and provided a challenge for men of ability, aggressiveness, and daring.

Jewish gangsters saw what they were doing in the same way that many of their non-Jewish colleagues saw themselves: they were providing a service. People wanted liquor, narcotics, gambling, and women. The gangster furnished them. And physical violence was accepted as a tool of the trade. It was a way to eliminate competition and protect one's interests.

At a time when Jews in Europe were at the mercy of hostile governments and under constant threat of violence and pogroms, the gangster provided American Jews with secret vicarious satisfaction and pride. In the complexities of the times, a number of Jewish gangsters acquired respect because they assumed the role of protector and defender of their people.

Despite their aversion to the gangster, even Jewish leaders were not above using their services on behalf of the community. Arnold Rothstein was asked to help end the New York garment district strike of 1926. Jewish "thugs" broke up numerous German-American Bund rallies in New York and New Jersey in the 1930s, and Jewish gangsters were asked to help secure arms during Israel's War of Independence (1948).

In spite of their own success in crime, most Jewish gangsters kept their families separate and away from being implicated in their criminal enterprises. West Coast mobster Mickey Cohen summarized this attitude when he said, "We had a code of ethics that one never involved his wife or family in his work." These men wanted their children to marry well and achieve respectability and acceptance in the legitimate world. Thus, they sent their children to the best schools and encouraged them to enter the professions such as law and medicine. In this, they were very much like many other Jewish parents of their generation. They described themselves as businessmen, building a network of illegal activities that included gambling, prostitution, smuggling, extortion, and protection money. They grew up in the Jewish ghettos of

America. They sent their children to college, rather than to the streets.

Few of these men were religiously observant. They rarely attended services, although they did support congregations financially. They did not keep kosher or send their children to day schools. However, at crucial moments they protected other Jews, in America, and around the world.

I'm not trying to paint these gangsters as heroes. There is absolutely no justification for the acts of these men. Their lives of crime are inexcusable. They committed acts of great evil. *They were not nice people.*

While many Jews today are sensitive to these kind of stories about crime, we should be more mature about their reality. We are not always perfect or a "Light to the Nations." But in some strange, twisted way, these men helped change the stereotypical portrait of the Jew. The horrors and images of dead, degraded Jews being bulldozed into mass graves, gave birth to another image closer to home. Tough, fearless, and often ungoverned except by their own boldness, these were Jews with guns, who recreated organized crime as a business blueprint for unimaginable success.

A.S. Winston

GOD GAVE US THE GARDEN OF EDEN. WE GAVE THE WORLD LAS VEGAS.

Dream City. Sin City. A desert DisneyWorld for grown-ups. Call it what you want, Las Vegas is a film set in its own right, an outdoor museum of American culture. There's no sense in insisting on logic when you're staying in a pyramid, which is down the street from the Statue of Liberty, which is a few doors up from the canals of Venice, which is across the street from a volcano, which has a view of the Eiffel Tower, from where you can watch pirates battle seductresses in a tiny lagoon, and though you're in the middle of the desert, the waters dance to an operatic syncopation, all under the watchful eye of Julius Caesar. When you're in Las Vegas, you need to let go. Reason must be abandoned.

Las Vegas is our nation's premier smorgasbord of sensation, the last frontier when it comes to ritualized excess. It is a city that provides a temporary sense of bravado, and a defiance of the ordinary, where 48 million people keep coming back year after year. Not bad for an old railroad town that parlayed legalized gambling (started in 1931), a federal construction boon (the Hoover Dam started that very same year), and mob invasion (Bugsy Siegel opened the Flamingo in 1946) into a perfect storm of tourism. It was all made mainstream when corporate investment in gambling was finally allowed in the 1960s.

This is a fantasy world, a place where you can have a good time, leave your cares behind, celebrate freedom, and go to the very edge of what's legal. It is a city that genuinely adores nonsense (Elvis is everywhere), cultivates the amazement of its visitors, and most of all, believes in everyone's right to buy fun. Freedom of individual spirit drives the city, not just entertainment and gambling. Though gambling has always been the big draw here, there is that indefinable quality that once you step into this town you get that certain "feeling" of excitement that is unmatched anywhere else. It is that no limit landscape of the mind that allows the people who visit (and live) here, to unleash their personal powers, whatever they are and wherever they may take them. That is the spirit of Las Vegas. It is also our gift to the world.

Shimmering from the desert haze of Nevada like a latter-day El Dorado, Las Vegas is the most dynamic, spectacular city on earth. At the start of the 20th century, it didn't even exist; now its home to two million people, and boasts a majority of the world's largest hotels.

A desert metropolis built on gambling, vice, and other forms of entertainment in just a century of existence, Las Vegas has drawn millions of visitors and trillions of dollars in wealth to southern Nevada. The city's embrace of Old West-style freedoms, gambling and prostitution, provided a perfect home for East Coast organized crime.

Beginning in the 1940s, money from drugs and racketeering built casinos and was laundered within them. Visitors came to partake in what the casinos offered: low-cost luxury and the thrill of fantasies fulfilled.

The mob associated with Las Vegas grew out of the "Great Migration" through Ellis Island. These immigrants and their next generation faced the same problems previous and future immigrants faced. Discrimination often deprived them of respectable, well-paying jobs. Accordingly, some turned to illegal activities: bootlegging, protection, prostitution, and gambling. Las Vegas was just waiting for them.

Jews first arrived in southern Nevada in 1850, attracted by the discovery of gold in Carson City. Their numbers grew after the establishment of a railway hub linking Phoenix, Salt Lake City, and southern California.

Vegas Jewry received a major boost in 1946, when Meyer Lansky, "Bugsy" Siegel, Moe Dalitz, Gus Greenbaum, Dave Berman, Morris Lansburgh, Morris Rosen, Sam Cohen, and other well-known, rather notorious, underworld figures helped kick-start the transformation of this otherwise sleepy desert rest stop into the nation's "vice and dice" capital. Las Vegas quickly became a Jewish mob town.

Love 'em or hate 'em, Jewish mobsters played a major role in Las Vegas' rise to becoming a renowned tourist destination. In its heyday, the mob controlled every Strip resort that was worth controlling, stealing untold millions of dollars. Despite claims by some Vegas old-timers that the town was much better when the mob ran it, these "luminaries" were no heroes.

It was Meyer Lansky who decided to capitalize on the cash cow Las Vegas would become. Before his arrival, "Sin City" was nothing more than a small desert town inhabited by cowboys and a few slot machines. And his timing couldn't have been better. Before Vegas,

American tourists looking for a hedonistic good time had to travel to Cuba. In Cuba, gangsters were welcomed by the corrupt Batista regime, casinos were plentiful, and the profits rolled in. A little over a decade after the first casino opened in Las Vegas, Fidel Castro's revolution swept through Cuba, and the party was over.

Thanks to the money made in Cuba, modern Vegas was essentially built on the mob's dime. Lansky, not wanting to be the one blamed if the Vegas plan didn't pan out, enlisted Bugsy Siegel, whose job was to drum up cash and enthusiasm among gangsters over the glitzy venture. Of course, Vegas boomed and Lansky took all the credit while Siegel got five bullets to the head (or wherever) for skimming on casino funds (you saw the movie, didn't you?).

The city attracted Jewish mobsters because the casinos were under-regulated at the time, and functioned as an almost inexhaustible "golden goose." To the "Kosher Mafia," even more than their Italian and Irish counterparts, the desert offered an almost unique opportunity to transcend criminal origins and reputations, and to achieve a modicum of communal and civic respectability. Many began this rehabilitative process by joining synagogues and funding parochial schools.

In 1970, Moe Dalitz, "a leading member of the Cleveland crime syndicate," and controller of the Stardust and Desert Inn Las Vegas casinos, was awarded the City of Peace Award of the State of Israel "in recognition of distinguished service to the people and state of Israel." In 1985 the Anti-Defamation League of B'nai B'rith bestowed their "Torch of Liberty" award upon him for his cash support of that group. One of the city's Jewish day schools, Temple Ner Tamid, was named for him. A gangster associate revealed to a 1947 organized crime commission that Dalitz was in fact the chairman of the Nevada United Jewish Appeal. Moe Dalitz and partners also famously built, with a Teamsters loan, the Sunrise Hospital and Medical Center. In 1982, Dalitz was listed by Forbes magazine as one of the 400 wealthiest people in America. In terms of the criminal underworld, he was also known as "the godfather of Las Vegas."

In the popular imagination, Las Vegas and the mob are joined at the hip. Their shared history is a point of fascination for many, thanks in no small part to movies such as "The Godfather," "Bugsy," and "Casino," which mytholized the role of organized crime in the city's creation and rise to glory.

The Flamingo was the first hotel to go up in 1946, though things got off to a "shaky start." After the Siegel fiasco, Lansky took over operations at the Flamingo and turned its fortune around, setting the stage for more of the mob in Las Vegas. Within a few years, the Thunderbird, Desert Inn, Sahara, Riviera, Dunes, Stardust, Caesar's Palace, and Sands were all open and drawing huge crowds with their lures of gambling and A-list performers. It was a non-stop, twenty-four hour a day party that lasted almost 30 years.

Organized crime was driven out of Vegas during the 1970s and 1980s. The mob's defeat began when eccentric billionaire Howard Hughes snapped up a slew of casinos in the 1960s, moving from top-floor penthouse to top-floor penthouse to call home, before settling on the Desert Inn. When profits failed to roll in as he'd hoped, he pushed to have local laws changed, allowing corporations to own casinos in Las Vegas. Those mobsters that weren't included in the first wave of casino buyouts, were included in the second wave in the early 1970s. With the mob driven out, Las Vegas was ready for a face change. Enter a new wave of Jewish entrepreneurs.

Steve Wynn spearheaded the dramatic expansion of Sin City, as well as it's resurgence with the building of the Mirage, the Golden Nugget, Treasure Island, Bellagio, the Wynn, and the Encore hotels and casinos (the funds for Wynn's first casino, the Golden Nugget, was in large part raised by Jewish financier Michael Milken).

Jay Sarno developed Caesar's Palace, Circus Circus, and the Imperial Palace Hotel (renamed the Quad Resort and Casino in 2012)

Sam Nazarian acquired the Sahara Hotel and Casino.

Sheldon Adelson became Chairman and CEO of the Las Vegas Sands Corp., the parent company of the Venetian Resort Hotel Casino, the Palazzo, and the Sands Expo and Convention Center.

Brian Greenspun was joint owner of Green Valley Ranch Resort and Casino, and Alliante Station.

Arthur Goldberg was the CEO of Park Place Entertainment: Caesar's Palace, Bally's, the Flamingo, and the Paris Hotel and Casino.

Bernie Rothkopf owned the MGM Hotel.

Jerome Mack, past president of the Dunes and Riviera, was a former national chairman of the Israel Bonds Campaign.

The Las Vegas mayor, Oscar Goodman, elected in 1999, was the former president of Temple Beth Sholom. He also had a reputation as a "mob lawyer," defending, among others, Meyer Lansky. His wife, Carolyn Goodman, is currently the Mayor of Las Vegas.

Herman "Hank" Greenspun, publisher of the Las Vegas Sun, once noted that he was a Zionist "before I could even identify a picture of George Washington." During Israel's "War of Independence" in 1948, Greenspun traveled to Mexico, the Dominican Republic, Guatemala, and Panama, where he organized false documents, bank guarantees, and arms shipments to Israel. He embarked on an incredible odyssey, plundering a naval depot in Hawaii, seizing a private yacht at gunpoint near Wilmington, California, and posing in Mexico as a confidential agent of Generalissimo Chiang Kai-Shek's government. His single driving purpose generated over the span of seven months regarding all those seemingly unrelated events was to fill the holds of a ship with six thousand tons of contraband rifles, machine guns, howitzers, cannons, and ammunition, destined for the port of Haifa and Israel's beleaguered Jews. In so doing, Hank Greenspun had violated the United States' Neutrality Act, the Export Control Law, and Presidential Proclamation 2776. Thanks to Jewish lobbying pressure, Greenspun was pardoned by President John F. Kennedy in 1961.

Vegas in the '50s and '60s was indeed another world. Those were the days of true escapism, when small-time gamblers came to town with their wives for a weekend of shows and great food. When you could ride down the elevator at one of the Strip hotels with Lucille Ball, have an A table at the Versailles Room at the Riviera to see Rowan and Martin, with Edie Adams opening, and laugh until it hurt when Buddy Hackett played the old Congo Room at the Sahara.

Today, Las Vegas is a mature playground (still family friendly, though that's definitely not the city's image), a highly hospitable travel destination, with plenty of opportunities to lose your inhibitions, and happily lose your money. Casinos are now not just gambling havens, but mega-resorts, complete with fun-filled attractions for the kids and luxuries such as spas, world-class dining, and "all kinds of entertainment." However, the colorful history of the Jewish mafia involvement remains. There's even a museum there dedicated to it.

A QUOTE IS JUST A TATTOO ON THE TONGUE

"Israel was not created in order to disappear. Israel will endure and flourish. It is the child of hope and the home of the brave. It can neither be broken by adversity nor demoralized by success. It carries the shield of democracy and it honors the sword of freedom."
-- John F. Kennedy, President of the United States

"I had faith in Israel before it was established, I have faith in it now. I believe it has a glorious future before it - not just another sovereign nation, but as an embodiment of the great ideals of our civilization."
-- Harry S. Truman, President of the United States

"I cannot imagine a greater expression of Christianity than to say, 'I, too, am a Jew.
--Barack Obama, President of the United States

"America and Israel share a special bond. Our relationship is unique among all nations. Like America, Israel is a strong democracy, a symbol of freedom, and an oasis of liberty, a home to the oppressed and persecuted."
-- William J. Clinton, President of the United States

"Our society is illuminated by the spiritual insights of the Hebrew prophets. America and Israel have a common love of human freedom, and they have a common faith in a democratic way of life."
-- Lyndon B. Johnson, President of the United States

"My commitment to the security and future of Israel is based upon basic morality as well as enlightened self-interest. Our role in supporting Israel honors our own heritage."
-- Gerald R. Ford, President of the United States

"...it would be a mistake...to ascribe to Roman legal conceptions an undivided sway over the development of law and institutions during the Middle Ages... The Laws of Moses as well as the laws of Rome contributed suggestions and impulse to the men and institutions which were to prepare the modern world; and if we could have but eyes to see... we should readily discover how very much besides religion we owe to the Jew."
--Woodrow Wilson, President of the United States

"I believe what Paul taught in Galatians, that there is no distinction in God's eyes between men and women, slaves and masters, Jews and non-Jews - everybody is created equally in the eyes of God."
--Jimmy Carter, President of the United States

"I will insist the Hebrews have [contributed] more to civilize men than any other nation. If I was an atheist and believed in blind eternal fate, I should still believe that fate had ordained the Jews to be the most essential instrument for civilizing the nations. They are the most

glorious nation that ever inhabited this Earth. The Romans and their empire were but a bubble in comparison to the Jews. They have given religion to three-quarters of the globe and have influenced the affairs of mankind more and more happily than any other nation, ancient or modern."

--John Adams, Second President of the United States, from a letter to F.A. Van der Kemp (Feb. 16, 1808), Pennsylvania Historical Society

"The Jew is that sacred being who has brought down from heaven the everlasting fire, and has illumined with it the entire world. He is the religious source, spring, and fountain out of which all the rest of the peoples have drawn their beliefs and their religions."

-- Leo Tolstoy

"The Talmud is to this day the circulating heart's blood of the Jewish religion. Whatever laws, customs, or ceremonies we observe, whether we are Orthodox, Conservative, Reform, or merely spasmodic sentimentalists, we follow the Talmud. It is our common law."

--Herman Wouk, author

"I am a Jew: Hath not a Jew eyes? Hath not a Jew hands, organs, dimensions, senses, affections, passions? Fed with the same food, hurt with the same weapons, subject to the same diseases, healed by the same means, warmed and cooled by the same winter and summer, as a Christian is?"

--William Shakespeare

"We can hardly get up in the morning or cross the street without being Jewish. We dream Jewish dreams and hope Jewish hopes. Most of our best words, in fact - new, adventure, surprise; unique, individual, person, vocation; time, history, future; freedom, progress, spirit; faith, hope, justice - are the gifts of the Jews."
--Henry Cahill

"One of the gifts of the Jewish culture to Christianity is that it has taught Christians to think like Jews, and any modern man who has not learned to think as though he were a Jew can hardly be said to have learned to think at all."
-- William Rees-Mogg, former Editor-in-Chief for The Times of London and a member of the House of Lords

"It is certain that in certain parts of the world we can see a peculiar people, separated from the other peoples of the world and this is called the Jewish people. This people is not only of remarkable antiquity but has also lasted for a singular long time. For whereas the people of Greece and Italy, of Sparta, Athens and Rome and others who came so much later have perished so long ago, these still exist, despite the efforts of so many powerful kings who have tried a hundred times to wipe them out, as their historians testify, and as can easily be judged by the natural order of things over such a long spell of years. They have always been preserved, however, and their preservation was foretold. My encounter with this people amazes me..."
--Blaise Pascal, French Mathematician

"The Jewish vision became the prototype for many similar grand designs for humanity, both divine and manmade The Jews, therefore, stand at the center of the perennial attempt to give human life the dignity of a purpose."
--Paul Johnson, American Historian

"As long as the world lasts, all who want to make progress in righteousness will come to Israel for inspiration as to the people who had the sense for righteousness most glowing and strongest."
--Matthew Arnold, British poet and critic.

"If there is any honor in all the world that I should like, it would be to be an honorary Jewish citizen."
--A.L Rowse, authority on Shakespeare

"Energy is the basis of everything. Every Jew, no matter how insignificant, is engaged in some decisive and immediate pursuit of a goal... It is the most perpetual people of the earth..."
--Johann Wolfgang von Goethe. German dramatist, novelist and poet

"Our forces saved the remnants of the Jewish people of Europe for a new life and a new hope in the reborn land of Israel. Along with all men of good will, I salute the young state and wish it well."
-- General Dwight D. Eisenhower

"If we were forced to choose just one, there would be no way to deny that Judaism is the most important intellectual development in human history."
--David Gelernter, Yale University Professor

"The Jews started it all—and by 'it' I mean so many of the things we care about, the underlying values that make all of us, Jew and Gentile, believer and aethiest, tick. Without the Jews, we would see the world through different eyes, hear with different ears, even feel with different feelings ... we would think with a different mind, interpret all our experience differently, draw different conclusions from the things that befall us. And we would set a different course for our lives."
--Thomas Cahill, The Gifts of The Jews

"The Jews, however, are beyond all doubt the strongest, toughest, and purest race at present living in Europe; they know how to succeed even under the worst conditions. The resourcefulness of the modern Jews, both in mind and soul, is extraordinary..."
--Friedrich Nietzsche, German Philosopher

"So prominent was the Jewish role in the foreign commerce of Europe that those nations that received the Jews gained and the countries that excluded them lost in the volume of international trade."
-- Will Durant, the Story of Civilization - The Reformation. (New York: Simon & Shuster, 1953)

"The preservation of the Jews is really one of the most signal and illustrious acts of divine Providence... and what but a supernatural power could have preserved them

in such a manner as none other nation upon earth hath been preserved. Nor is the providence of God less remarkable in the destruction of their enemies, than in their preservation... We see that the great empires, which in their turn subdued and oppressed the people of God, are all come to ruin... And if such hath been the fatal end of the enemies and oppressors of the Jews, let it serve as a warning to all those, who at any time or upon any occasion are for raising a clamor and persecution against them."

--Thomas Newton - British Clergyman: Bishop of Bristol (1704-1782)

"Certainly, the world without the Jews would have been a radically different place. Humanity might have eventually stumbled upon all the Jewish insights. But we cannot be sure. All the great conceptual discoveries of the human intellect seem obvious and inescapable once they had been revealed, but it requires a special genius to formulate them for the first time. The Jews had this gift. To them we owe the idea of equality before the law, both divine and human; of the sanctity of life and the dignity of human person; of the individual conscience and so a personal redemption; of collective conscience and so of social responsibility; of peace as an abstract ideal and love as the foundation of justice, and many other items which constitute the basic moral furniture of the human mind. Without Jews it might have been a much emptier place."

--Paul Johnson - Christian historian, author of A History of the Jews and A History of Christianity

"No ancient people have had a stranger history than the Jews. ... The history of no ancient people should be so valuable, if we could only recover it and understand it. ... Stranger still, the ancient religion of the Jews survives, when all the religions of every ancient race of the pre-Christian world have disappeared ... Again it is strange that the living religions of the world all build on religious ideas derived from the Jews. .... The great matter is not "What happened?" but "Why did it happen?" Why does Judaism live?"

--T.R. Glover, (The Ancient World, Penguin)

"What is the Jew?...What kind of unique creature is this whom all the rulers of all the nations of the world have disgraced and crushed and expelled and destroyed; persecuted, burned and drowned, and who, despite their anger and their fury, continues to live and to flourish. What is this Jew whom they have never succeeded in enticing with all the enticements in the world, whose oppressors and persecutors only suggested that he deny (and disown) his religion and cast aside the faithfulness of his ancestors? The Jew is the symbol of eternity. He is the one who for so long had guarded the prophetic message and transmitted it to all mankind. A people such as this can never disappear. The Jew is eternal. He is the embodiment of eternity."

--Leo Tolstoy

"The Jews were the first people to develop an integrated view of life and its obligations. Rather than imagining the demands of law and the demands of wisdom as discrete realms (as did the Sumerians, the Egyptians, and the Greeks), they imagined that all of life,

having come from the Author of life, was to be governed by a single outlook. The material and the spiritual, the intellectual and the moral were one."

--Thomas Cahill, The Gifts of the Jews

"There is a striking point that runs through Jewish history as a whole. Western civilization was born in the Middle East, and the Jews were at its crossroads. In the heyday of Rome, the Jews were close to the Empire's center. When power shifted eastward, the Jewish center was in Babylon; when it skipped to Spain, there again were the Jews. When in the Middle Ages the center of civilization moved into Central Europe, the Jews were waiting for it in Germany and Poland. The rise of the United States to the leading world power found Judaism focused there. And now, today, when the pendulum seems to be swinging back toward the Old World and the East rises to renewed importance, there again are the Jews in Israel..."

--Professor Huston Smith, The Religions of Man, New York: HarperCollins, 1989

"Who has made us Jews different from all other people? Who has allowed us to suffer so terribly up until now? It is God who has made us as we are, but it will be God, too, who will raise us up again. Who knows it might even be our religion from which the world and all peoples learn 'good,' and for that reason and only that reason do we suffer. We can never become just Netherlanders, or just English or representatives of any country for that matter. We will always remain Jews."

- - From the diary of Anne Frank, April 11, 1944

"Of all the extreme fanaticism which plays havoc in man's nature, there is not one as irrational as anti-Semitism."
--Lloyd George, stated in 1923

"Israel's great achievement, so apparent that mention of it is almost trite, was Monotheism. It was an achievement that transformed subsequent history....One may raise the question whether any other single contribution from whatever source since human culture emerged from the stone age has had the far reaching effect upon history that Israel in this regard has exerted both through the mediums of Christianity and Islam and directly through the world of Jewish thinkers themselves"
--from The Intellectual Adventure of Ancient Man, by H. and H. A. Frankfort, John A. Wilson, Thorkild Jacobsen, William A. Irwin

"If the statistics are right, the Jews constitute but one percent of the human race. It suggests a nebulous dim puff of star dust lost in the blaze of the Milky Way. Properly the Jew ought hardly to be heard of, but he is heard of, has always been heard of. He is as prominent on the planet as any other people, and his commercial importance is extravagantly out of proportion to the smallness of his bulk. His contributions to the world's list of great names in literature, science, art, music, finance, medicine, and abstruse learning are also away out of proportion to the weakness of his numbers."
--Mark Twain

"The Jews are a peculiar people: Things permitted to other nations are forbidden to the Jews. Other nations

drive out thousands, even millions of people, and there is no refugee problem. Russia did it. Poland and Czechoslovakia did it. Turkey threw out a million Greeks and Algeria a million Frenchmen. Indonesia threw out heaven knows how many Chinese, and no one says a word about refugees. But in the case of Israel, the displaced Arabs have become eternal refugees. Everyone insists that Israel must take back every single Arab. Arnold Toynbee calls the displacement of the Arabs an atrocity greater than any committed by the Nazis. Other nations when victorious on the battlefield dictate peace terms. But when Israel is victorious it must sue for peace. Everyone expects the Jews to be the only real Christians in this world."

--Eric Hoffer, author, philosopher

"The Jews who will it shall achieve their State. We shall live at last as free men on our own soil, and in our own homes peacefully die. The world will be liberated by our freedom, enriched by our wealth, magnified by our greatness. And whatever we attempt there for our own benefit will redound mightily and beneficially to the good of all mankind."

--Theodor Herzl, father of modern Zionism

Asked why he, a Gentile, was donating one million dollars to the Aish Ha Torah's World Outreach Center in Jerusalem, the successful American entrepreneur John Kluge responded: *"Last year I turned 80 years old. At my birthday party, I realized 85% of my friends are Jews. I have always admired the Jewish people and their contributions to humanity, to civilizing the World. What Aish Ha Torah is doing to reconnect Jews with their heritage, to strengthen their roots, to educate them of their values, is enabling the Jewish people to be able to play their incredibly valuable role in history."*

SAY IT LOUD, AND SAY IT PROUD!

A.S. Winston

THE MEDIA IS OFTEN CONSIDERED THE MOUTHPIECE OF MODERN CULTURE

It makes no sense at all to try to deny the reality of Jewish prominence in popular culture. But do we control the media? Well, "let's dust off our crystal ball and look back into the last century" to understand how such beliefs were born.

The Newhouse media empire was founded by the late Samuel Newhouse, an immigrant from Russia. When he died in 1979 at the age of 84, he bequeathed media holdings worth $1.3 billion to his two sons, Samuel and Donald. Since then, with a number of additional acquisitions, the net worth of his empire has grown to more than $8 billion today.

Samuel Newhouse, Jr. and Donald Newhouse own 31 daily newspapers, including the Cleveland Plain Dealer, the Newark Star-Ledger, and the New Orleans Times-Picayune; they also own the nation's largest trade book publishing conglomerate, Random House, with all its subsidiaries. Newhouse Broadcasting consists of 12 television broadcasting stations and 87 cable-TV systems, including some of the country's largest cable networks. They also own the Sunday supplement, Parade, with a circulation of more than 22 million copies per week, and some two dozen major magazines, including the New Yorker, Vogue, Mademoiselle, Glamour, Vanity Fair, HQ, Bride's, Gentlemen's Quarterly, Self, and Home and Garden.

Nationally, over 56 million newspapers are sold daily in our nation. On Sunday, over 60 million are sold. The New York Times, the Wall Street Journal, and the Washington Post, are the newspapers that set the guidelines for almost all others. The Sulzberger family owns the New York Times, and through the New York Times Co., 36 other newspapers, and twelve magazines, including McCall's and Family Circle.

New York Mayor Mortimer Zuckerman owns the New York Daily News, as well as U.S. News and World Report.

The New York Post is owned by billionaire Jewish real estate developer Peter Kalikow.

The Village Voice is the personal property of Leonard Stern.

There are only three magazines of any note published in the United States: Time, Newsweek, and U.S. News and World Report.

Newsweek, as mentioned above, is published by the Washington Post Co., under the guidance of Katherine Meyer Graham.

The CEO of Time Warner Communications is Steven J. Ross.

U.S. News and World Report is owned and published by Jewish real estate developer Mortimer B. Zuckerman.

The three largest book publishers, Random House, Simon & Schuster, and Time Inc. Book Co. are owned by Jews.

Western Publishing ranks first among publishers of children's books, with more than 50% of the market. It's chairman and CEO is Richard Bernstein.

A media conglomerate, media group, or media institution is a company that owns numerous companies involved in mass media enterprises, such as television, radio, publishing, motion pictures, theme parks, or the Internet. Among the largest of these is the Walt Disney Company, whose chairman and CEO, Robert Iger, is a Jew. The Disney Empire includes several television production companies (Walt Disney Television, Touchstone Television, Buena Vista Television), its own cable network, and two video production companies. As for feature films, the Walt Disney Picture Group headed by Joe Roth, includes Walt Disney Pictures *(Beauty and the Beast, Frozen, Moana, The Jungle Book, Pirates of the Caribbean)*, Touchstone Pictures, Hollywood Pictures, Lucasfilm *(Star Wars, Indiana Jones)*, Marvel Studios *(Hulk, Spiderman, Iron Man, Thor, Guardians of the Galaxy, Captain America, the Avengers)*. Disney also owns Pixar *(Toy Story, Finding Nemo, Cars, Finding Dory, WALL-E)*.

The company's resorts and diversified related holdings include Walt Disney Parks and Resorts, Disneyland Resort, Walt Disney World Resort, Tokyo Disney Resort, Disneyland Paris, Euro Disney S.C.A., Hong Kong Disneyland Resort, Shanghai Disney Resort, Disney Vacation Club, and the Disney Cruise Line.

Disney also sells well over a billion dollars of consumer products annually.

In August, 1995, Michael Eisner (Disney chairman and CEO at the time) acquired Capital Cities/ABC, Inc., to create a media empire with annual sales of $16.5 billion. Capital Cities/ABC owns the ABC Television Network, which in turn owns ten TV stations outright, in such big markets as New York, Chicago, Philadelphia, Los Angeles, and Houston. In addition, it has 225 affiliated stations in the U.S. and is part owner of several European TV companies.

ABC's cable subsidiary, ESPN, is headed by president and CEO Steven Bornstein. The corporation also has a controlling share of Lifetime Television, and the A&E Network cable companies. ABC Radio Network owns 11 AM and 10 FM stations, again in major cities (New York, Washington, D.C., and Los Angeles), and has over 3,400 affiliates. Although primarily a telecommunications company, Capital Cities/ABC also earns over $1 billion annually in publishing, owning seven daily newspapers, plus Fairchild Publications (Women's Wear Daily), Chilton Publications (automotive manuals), and the Diversified Publishing Group.

Gerald Levin and Steven Ross were the "deal makers" making Time Warner, Inc. the second of the international media leviathons. Time Warner's subsidiary HBO is the country's largest pay-TV cable network. Warner Music is by far the world's largest music company with 50 labels, the biggest of which is Warner Brothers Music. In addition to cable and music, Time Warner is heavily involved in the production of feature films (Warner Brothers Studio), and publishing. Time Warner's publishing division is the largest magazine publisher in the country (Time, Sports Illustrated, People, Fortune).

Viacom, Inc., headed by Sumner Redstone (born Murray Rothstein), is the third largest megamedia corporation in the country, with revenues in excess of $10 billion a year. Viacom, which produces and distributes TV programs for the three largest networks, also owns 12 television stations and 12 radio stations. It produces feature films through Paramount Pictures, once headed by Sherry Lansing, now headed by Brad Grey. Its publishing division include Prentice Hall, Simon & Schuster, and Pocket Books. At one time it distributed videos through 4,000 Blockbuster stores. It is also involved in satellite broadcasting, theme parks, and video games. Viacom Media Networks is the largest portfolio of cable networks in the United States, in terms of audience share. It is also among the most vibrant, diverse and culturally relevant collection of brands in media and entertainment.

MTV is the world's premiere youth entertainment brand. With a global reach of more than a half-billion households, MTV is the cultural home of the millennial generation, music fans and artists, and a pioneer in creating innovative programming for young people, being a dominant influence on teenagers around the world. Nickelodeon's U.S. television network is seen in more than 90 million households and has been the number-one-rated basic cable network for 20 consecutive years. Nickelodeon has by far the largest share of the 4 to 11 year old TV audience in America, and is rapidly expanding through Europe. Available on-air, online and on-the-go, Comedy Central provides its audience access to the cutting-edge, laugh-out-loud world of comedy wherever and whenever they want it. Comedy Central is the number one brand in comedy. BET is the primary channel of BET Networks, the nation's leading provider of quality entertainment, music, news and public affairs television programming for the African-American audience and all who celebrate black culture. BET reaches more than 90 million households and can be seen in the United States, Canada, the Caribbean, the United Kingdom and sub-Saharan Africa.

All under the Viacom umbrella.

Most of the television and movie production companies that are not owned by the largest corporations are also controlled by Jews. For example, New World Entertainment, proclaimed by one media analyst as "the premiere independent TV program producer in the United States," is owned by Ronald Perelman, who also owns Revlon cosmetics.

The best known of the smaller media companies, Dreamworks SKG, is a strictly kosher affair. Dreamworks was formed in 1994 amid great media hype by recording industry mogul, David Geffen, former Disney Pictures chairman, Jeffrey Katzenberg, and film director Steven Spielberg, all three of whom are Jews. The company produces movies, animated films (*Shrek, Madagascar, Kung Fu Panda, How to Train Your Dragon*), television programs, and recorded music.

Two other large production companies, MCA and Universal Pictures, are both owned by Seagram Company, Ltd. The president and CEO of Seagram, the liquor giant, is Edgar Bronfman, Jr., who is also president of the World Jewish Congress.

The big three in television network broadcasting used to be ABC, NBC, and CBS. With the consolidation of the media empires, these three are no longer independent entities. While they were independent, however, each was controlled by a Jew through the years: ABC by Leonard Goldenson; CBS first by William Paley, and then by Lawrence Tisch; and NBC, first by David Sarnoff, and then by his son Robert.

The Jewish presence in television news remains particularly strong. As noted, ABC is part of the Walt Disney Company, and the executive producers of ABCs news programs are all Jews *(20/20, Good Morning America, World News Tonight).* CBS was purchased by Westinghouse Electric Corp. Nevertheless, the president of CBS news is also Jewish. At NBC, now owned by General Electric Co, the Jewish presence hasn't changed. The president of NBC News, and the executive producers of *Today, NBC Nightly News,* and *Dateline*, are all Jews.

After television news, the daily newspaper is the most influential information medium in America. Newspapers are not supported by their subscribers (well, maybe just a little bit), but by their advertisers. It is advertising revenue that largely covers their expenses and salaries, and yields the owner's profit. Since the beginning of the 20th century, when Jewish mercantile power in America became a dominant economic force, there has been a steady rise in the number of American newspapers owned by Jews (Jewish merchants supporting Jewish businessmen…those two pennies definitely have special powers).

The New York Times was founded in 1851 by Henry J. Raymond and George Jones. After their deaths, it was purchased in 1896 from Jones' estate by a wealthy Jewish publisher, Adolph Ochs. His great-grandson, Arthur Ochs Sulzberger, Jr. is the paper's current publisher and CEO. The executive editor is Max Frankel, and the managing editor is Joseph Lelyveld, both of whom are Jews.

The Sulzberger family also owns, through the New York Times Co., 33 other newspapers, including the Boston Globe, purchased in 1993 for $1.1 billion; twelve magazines, including McCall's and Family Circle (with circulations of more than 5 million each); seven radio and TV broadcasting stations, a cable TV system, and three book publishing companies. The New York Times News Service transmits news stories, features, and photographs from the New York Times, by wire to more than 500 other newspapers, news agencies and magazines.

Of similar national importance is the Washington Post. Like the New York Times, the Washington Post had a non-Jewish origin. It was established in 1877 by Stilson Hutchins, purchased from him in 1905 by John R.McLean, and later inherited by Edward B. McLean. In June, 1933, however, at the height of the Great Depression, the newspaper was forced into bankruptcy, where it was purchased at a bankruptcy auction by Eugene Meyer, a Jewish financier and former partner of Bernard Baruch, the industry czar in America during the First World War.

The Washington Post is now run by Kathryn Meyer Graham, Eugene Meyer's daughter. She is the principal stockholder and board chairman of the Washington Post Co.

The Washington Post Co. has a number of other media holdings in newspapers, television, and magazines, most notably the nation's number two weekly newsmagazine, Newsweek. And, in a joint venture with the New York Times, the Post publishes the International Herald Tribune, the most widely distributed English language daily in the world.

The Wall Street Journal, which sells 1.8 million copies each weekday, is the nation's largest-circulation daily newspaper. It is owned by Dow Jones & Company, Inc., a New York corporation which also publishes 24 other daily newspapers and the weekly financial tabloid, Barron's, among other things. The chairman and CEO of Dow Jones & Company is Peter R. Kahn (yes, Jewish). Kahn also holds the posts of chairman and publisher of the Wall Street Journal.

New York's other major newspapers (besides the New York Times and the Wall Street Journal) are also Jewish owned. The New York Daily News was bought from the estate of the late Jewish media mogul Robert Maxwell (born Ludvik Hoch), by Jewish real-estate developer Mortimer B. Zuckerman, once Mayor of New York City. The Village Voice is the personal property of Leonard Stern, the billionaire owner of the Hartz Mountain pet supply firm.

While our crystal ball has shown us the last century, it's time to return to the here and now.

Yes, we have a strong presence in the media. We also have a strong presence in medicine, science, math, physics, philanthropy, and the arts. Considering our small numbers, we are over-represented in many fields of learning and accomplishment. We are ambitious, curious, energetic, imaginative, persistent, goal-oriented, intelligent, and driven, all of which has helped us in our endeavors to follow our dreams and make them a reality.

There is no sinister sub-plot to our achievements. We work hard. We have visions. We set goals…and we succeed.

I believe we Jews have something planted in each one of us that makes us very different from every other group in the world. I'm talking about a group of people that were put in death camps, endured pogroms, and had their whole families decimated, then came to America, the one place that truly let them "flex their muscles" with all the freedoms they were so long denied. No other group in the world has overachieved as have the Jewish people. This ability to succeed, this inner drive, comes not just from years of education or any other sort of conditional factors, but because of an inner spark that refuses to die within each of us.

Our association with the media is well deserved, earned through hard work, a passion to succeed, and a lifetime dedicated to personal achievement.

For a minority consisting of *less* than two cents of the world's population, the question begs, why are we so massively and disproportionately represented in the media? One answer might be because much of the most popular media is created in our own backyard, specifically in the two parts of the USA with the highest per capita Jewish populations, Los Angeles and New York City. Another is because Jews believe that people are creators, not just consumers; the role of man (and woman) is to improve and perfect God's creations through work, and innovation (I know, I know, sounds like preaching from the bimah to me, too).

When you add Jewish success in finance, the economy, government, science, the medical profession, the legal profession, in fact all the professions, one has to come away amazed at how such staggering success has been acquired by such a microscopic percent of the world's 7.5 billion people.

Do we control the media? Let the rest of the world knock themselves out debating the matter. As I've indicated earlier, those Jews who work in media, those "media machers and mavens," have done so as individuals traveling their own personal paths, pursuing their own individual dreams, not solely as representatives of Judaism, and certainly not in any coordinated conspiratorial manner. Every single one of them, knew what they wanted to achieve with their lives. They believed in themselves, had mental toughness, worked hard and smart, and (I'm guessing), enjoyed the pursuit of those dreams with an incredible passion that brought them their success. These people are the living formula of .002 of 1% = 2 cents.

THIS IS AMERICA...WHERE WE CELEBRATE SUCCESS. WE DO NOT APOLOGIZE FOR IT!

LIFE WITHOUT LIBERTY IS LIKE A BODY WITHOUT SPIRIT

Jewish Americans were not just involved in nearly every important social movement, but in the forefront of promoting such issues as worker's rights, civil rights, woman's rights, gay rights, freedom of religion, freedom from religion, peace movements, and various other progressive causes.

N.O.W. (the National Organization for Women), NAACP (National Association for the Advancement of Colored People), JDL (Jewish Defense League), ACLU (American Civil Liberties Union), ADL (Anti-Defamation League), Planned Parenthood, B'nai B'rith, National Council of Christians and Jews, World Zionist Organization, Jewish World Federation, and the Simon Wiesenthal Center, are all Jewish founded organizations.

Today, American Jews are a distinctive and influential group in our nation's politics. We have the highest percentage voter turnout of any ethnic group. We tend to view politics in terms of social and economic redemption rather than as an opportunity for personal advancement. Largely excluded from the politics of Eastern Europe, most Jews did not believe politics was a place where a nice Jewish boy should pursue a career. Jews were influential in postwar American politics as intellectuals, contributors, and voters, but not as politicians. That was then. Times have changed. Though skeptical toward politicians, Jews are no longer skeptical of the political process. For them, it is a means to create a better world.

The role of campaign contributions given by Jews deserves special mention. Over 60 percent of the campaign funds collected by the Democratic Party and a respectable percentage of Republican campaign funds stem from Jewish sources.

The Washington Post once noted, *"In states such as Florida and New York, Jewish voters are a large enough percentage of voters to play a crucial role in election outcomes. In presidential elections, Democratic candidates depend on Jewish supporters to supply as much as 60 percent of the money raised from private sources. Any significant reduction in the financial support will weaken Democratic candidates and the Democratic Party organizations."*

In sum, we account for the majority of campaign contributions to the Democratic Party, and about 20% to 35% of campaign contributions to the Republican Party.

Eventually we realized campaign donations weren't enough. There was so much more that we could contribute, and with that objective in mind, we decided to "really get involved."

On the first Monday of October of every year, the Supreme Court, the highest court in the land, begins its term. The Supreme Court is composed of nine judges, known as Justices appointed to the Court by the President of the United States. The names of Louis Brandeis, Benjamin N. Cardozo, Abe Fortas, Felix Frankfurter,

Arthur J. Goldberg, Ruth Bader Ginsburg, Stephen Breyer, Sonia Sotomayor, and Elena Kagan, are all a permanent part of our American heritage.

We've served our country as Secretary of State, Secretary of Defense, Head of the National Security Council, Chairman of the Federal Reserve Bank, General Counsel for the FBI, White House Special Counsel, Secretary of Commerce, Secretary of Labor, Secretary of the Treasury, Secretary of Health, National Security Advisor, CIA Director, White House Press Secretary, Attorney General, Secretary of Transportation, Secretary of Commerce, White House Chief of Staff, Secretary of Agriculture, and Secretary for Homeland Security.

We've served as Ambassadors to the nations of Germany, France, Poland, Denmark, Hungary, Rumania, Belgium, Belarus, South Africa, India, Turkey, New Zealand, Egypt, Sweden, Mexico, Singapore, Zambia, Brazil, Bolivia, Canada, Cuba, Norway, Switzerland, Singapore, Spain, Slovakia, Laos, Thailand, Taiwan, Austria, Israel, Uruguay, the Soviet Union, Cyprus, Pakistan, Ethiopia, and the Ottoman Empire.

We've served as Governors in Georgia, Wisconsin, Washington, South Carolina, California, Idaho, Utah, New Mexico, Oregon, Illinois, New York, Alaska, Connecticut, Rhode Island, Maryland, Pennsylvania, Vermont, Virginia, Hawaii, Delaware, and Florida.

We've served as Senators for the states of Michigan, Pennsylvania, New Jersey, Wisconsin, Connecticut, California, Oregon, New York, Maryland, Delaware,

Vermont, Colorado, Minnesota, Florida, Louisiana, Arizona, Arkansas, Ohio, Nebraska, Maine, New Hampshire, Nevada, and Virginia.

We've served as Mayor for the cities of Atlanta, Beverly Hills, Boca Raton, Cincinnati, Dallas, Indianapolis, Hoboken, Iowa City, Kansas City, Las Vegas, Louisville, Miami, Minneapolis, New Orleans, New York, Phoenix, Philadelphia, Pittsburgh, Providence, Saint Paul, San Diego, San Francisco, Seattle, Worcester, Ventura, and both Portland, Maine, and Portland, Oregon.

The great success of America as a political structure (and nation) has resulted, in very large part, from the voluntary participation of its citizens in its public affairs; from taking part in political campaigns, to running for political office; from petitioning legislatures, to supporting the President in an hour of crisis; from assuming responsibility for the common good, to believing the Constitution has functioned well (most of the time), because conscientious men and women have given it flesh. And we are very proud to be an integral part of that process and their never ending American dream.

SAY IT LOUD, AND SAY IT PROUD!

THE ELEPHANT IN THE ROOM…

Some things just naturally go together, like salt and pepper, spaghetti and meatballs, cheese and crackers, Batman & Robin, Laurel & Hardy, Romeo and Juliet, peanut butter and jelly, horse and carriage, love and marriage, fish and chips, shoes and socks, sugar and spice, birds and bees, pen and paper, soap and water, gin and tonic, 'burger and fries, hugs and kisses, milk and cookies, life and death, Abbott and Costello, Mickey and Minnie, mac' and cheese, hammer and nails, bacon and eggs, table and chair, bread and butter, Sonny and Cher, Laverne and Shirley, Ozzie and Harriet, yin and yang, ebony and ivory, Mork and Mindy, war and peace, Bert and Ernie, Jews and money.

Jews and money. The subject will always be the elephant in the room. Yes, it's true. Jews are disproportionately successful in their endeavors, (remember those two pennies you're holding). We also make up more than twenty-five percent of the Forbes 400 list of the wealthiest people in the world; 48% of U.S. billionaires are Jewish; of the 25 billionaires living in New York City, 19 are Jewish; 46% of Jews in the United States make over $100,000 a year; 18% of Jewish households have a net worth of $1 million or more; more than 55% of all Jewish adults received a college degree and 25% earned a graduate degree. Though we often try to downplay Jewish success, facts are facts and the statistics don't lie.

When it comes to success and achievement, we Jews do punch higher than our weight, and as a result of that success, Jewish people get much more scrutiny than our relatively small population would normally account for (we're less than 2% of the U.S. population), especially when it comes to money.

The major reason for Jewish success can be directly traced to Torah. For millennia, sacred Jewish texts such as the Torah, have provided a unique view of the world, giving readers a particular sense of right and wrong, an ordering of priorities, and a way of doing things that reaches back to our founding fathers, Moses and Abraham. These ancient Jewish writings are amazing repositories of knowledge, containing powerful advice anyone can apply to success in business as well as any other aspect of their life. We Jews have absorbed the wisdom and teachings of the Torah for thousands of years (if not directly, then through osmosis). It's in our DNA.

One of the things people forget about history is that Jews were traditionally forced into roles as merchants and moneylenders in Christian nations because they weren't allowed to own land. In Medieval Europe, the "financial industry" was one of the only fields open to us. The Catholic Church preaches poverty as a virtue. Because of the Christian prohibition against usury, Jews found themselves an indispensable niche in their very small piece of the world.

Jews have been much more active in preserving their ethnic identity than any other immigrant group, creating an unparalleled web of charitable, cultural, and defense organizations. Philanthropy and good works, support for Israel, and Holocaust remembrance are just part of the core religion of American Jews.

Many Jewish people would rather reserve the subject of their success for private conversations (with the Internet these days, that's virtually impossible), believing their accomplishments might fuel the fires of anti-Semitism (unfortunately, too often they do). My personal feeling is that anti-Semitism isn't something that's acquired over the course of a lifetime. It's something you're born with. "It's in the mother's milk." We shouldn't feel uncomfortable about 5778 years of successful networking. And we certainly shouldn't have to apologize for it. We should embrace our accomplishments, and the financial success that accompanies it. So why not SAY IT LOUD AND SAY IT PROUD, and say it often?

BEFORE WE CELEBRATE ARTIFICIAL INTELLIGENCE WHY DON'T WE FIRST DO SOMETHING ABOUT NATURAL STUPIDITY?

"Money is the God of the Jews." Yeah, well, the Scotch are tight, the English are stuck up, blondes are dumb, the Irish love to drink, blacks like fried chicken and watermelon, Asians are good at math, all Arabs and Muslims are terrorists, all Italians are in the mafia, whites can't dance, all men are clueless, and don't even get me started on rednecks and politicians. Before we celebrate artificial intelligence why don't we first do something about natural stupidity?

"Tzedakah" is the Hebrew word for the acts that we call "charity" in English: giving aid, assistance, and money, to the poor and needy, or to other worthy causes. Tzedakah literally means "righteousness" in Hebrew. In the bible, tzedakah is used to refer to justice, kindness, ethical behavior and the like. This translation is consistent with Jewish thought, as Judaism considers charity to be an act of justice. Jews have a mandate to improve the world in which they live through the performance of good deeds. I know it sounds like another one of those Saturday morning sermons, but it isn't (there's that DNA thing again).

The nature of tzedakah is very different from the idea of charity. The word "charity" suggests benevolence and generosity, an altruistic act by the "haves" for the benefit of the "have nots." In Judaism, giving to the poor is not viewed as a magnanimous act; it is simply an act of justice and righteousness, the performance of a duty. And this obligation includes giving to both Jews and non-Jews alike.

Jews traditionally figure prominently among the country's (and world's) elite philanthropists. The Giving Pledge, a philanthropic initiative started by Warren Buffett and Bill and Melinda Gates, now has 158 members from around the world who have pledged to give away more than half of their assets during their lifetime, and more than half of these members are Jewish. Again I reiterate, contrary to popular belief, Jews do not just "take care of our own." Consider the following...

Larry Ellison was born to a 19 year old unwed Jewish mother, grew up with his great aunt, didn't even meet his mother till he was in his late 40s, and yet had the drive and ability to found the extraordinary computer software giant, Oracle. As of August 2017, he was listed by Forbes magazine as the fifth-wealthiest person in the United States and as the seventh-wealthiest in the world, with a fortune of $58 billion. He has already donated hundreds of millions of dollars to medical research and educational institutions in the U.S., and has responded to the call from Bill Gates and Warren Buffett, to publicly pledge his fortune to those less fortunate. *Tzedakah.*

Michael Bloomberg, once Mayor of New York City, and a former equity trader and partner in Salomon

Brothers, used some of his severance package (after being fired in 1981), to develop what became the global financial news and media company, Bloomberg, L.P. His success has allowed him to engage in substantial philanthropic endeavors (World Health Organization), including the donation of over $300 million to Johns Hopkins University, plus a combined donation of $500 million with Bill Gates to help governments in developing countries. *Tzedakah.*

The son of Polish Jewish immigrants who survived Nazi Europe and arrived in the United States practically penniless, Henry Samueli became interested in electronics and earned three degrees, including a Ph.D. in electrical engineering. In 1991, while working as a professor at UCLA, Samueli co-founded Broadcom Corporation, which has grown into a billion-dollar wireless and broadband communication business. The Samuelis have been known for their magnanimous philanthropic endeavors long before their latest commitment to the Giving Pledge. The couple established the Center for Integrative Medicine at the University of California, Irvine, and the Samueli Institute of Information Biology based in Washington, D.C. Henry and Susan Samueli have also supported the world renowned John Wayne Cancer Institute's ground-breaking research in the area of cancer prevention and treatment, which has already had a dramatic impact on cancer treatment. *Tzedakah.*

Elon Reeve Musk is a South African-born American business magnate, investor, engineer, and inventor. He is best known for his role as co-founder and head of product design at Tesla Motors. In 2001, Musk conceptualized

"Mars Oasis"; a project to land a miniature experimental greenhouse on Mars, containing food crops growing on the Martian landscape. In 2002, SpaceX (Space Exploration Technologies) was born as a private American aerospace manufacturer and space transport services company. It is the largest private producer of rocket engines in the world. His various endeavors and patents have made him one of the richest men on the planet. Elon Musk has joined the Giving Pledge. *Tzedakah.*

Moscow-born Sergei Brin is the co-founder, with Larry Page, of Google, the world's largest internet company, which they developed into their peerless search engine while roommates at Stanford University. With an estimated net worth of $46 billion, he wants to help solve the world's energy and climate problems, using Google's philanthropic arm, which invests in the alternative energy industry to find wider sources of renewable energy. The company acknowledges that its founders want "to solve really big problems using technology." *Tzedakah.*

Launching one of the world's richest science prizes, a foundation created by Silicon Valley tech luminaries awarded $3 million each to 11 health researchers studying stem cells, genetics, cancer and other diseases. The cash awards are more than double the size of those for the prestigious Nobel Prize. They were handed out at a San Francisco ceremony by the Breakthrough Prize in Life Sciences Foundation, which was created by Google co-founder Sergey Brin, Facebook founder Mark Zuckerberg, and Russian entrepreneur and venture capitalist Yuri Milner. The Breakthrough Prize in Life

Science is for recognizing excellence in research aimed at curing intractable disease and extending human life. *Tzedakah.*

Peter B. Lewis, a 1955 graduate and trustee of Princeton University, is the chairman and chief executive officer of Progressive Corporation, the fourth-largest personal auto insurer in the U.S. He has given $50 million to the Guggenheim Museum in New York, more to the ACLU, and another $300 million to his alma mater, Princeton University for a range of designated purposes. *Tzedakah.*

Lev Avnerovich Leviev is a Soviet-born Israeli businessman, philanthropist and investor. With a net worth of roughly $12 billion, Leviev is one of the most prominent Mizrahi Jewish individuals in the world and has been a major philanthropist for Hasidic Jewish causes in Eastern Europe and Israel. Leviev owns diamond mines in Russia and Africa, and is a major competitor to the DeBeers International diamond cartel. He reportedly donates at least $30 million each year to causes associated with the Hasidic movement. *Tzedakah.*

During his lifetime, it is estimated that Jewish publisher and diplomat Walter H. Annenberg donated over $2 billion. "Education," he once said, "holds civilization together". Many school buildings, libraries, theaters, hospitals, and museums across the United States now bear his name. His collection of French impressionist art was valued at approximately $1.38 billion in 1991 and was donated to the Metropolitan Museum of Art in New York City upon his death in 2002. In 1990, he donated

$50 million to the United Negro College Fund which was the largest amount ever contributed to the organization. *Tzedakah.*

After directing *Schindler's List,* Steven Spielberg started several foundations to support the Jewish community and survivors of the Holocaust, saying he could not keep the profits from the movie (now more than $321 million), "because it was blood money." Instead, he used it to create the Righteous Persons Foundation, which donates money to Jewish organizations and historical projects that relate to the Holocaust, and the Shoah Foundation, which has collected over 50,000 testimonials of people who lived through the Holocaust or experienced it firsthand, including Jews, Gypsies, homosexuals, and other minorities. It is now focused on its new mission of overcoming prejudice, intolerance, and bigotry. Additional Righteous Persons grants went to Brandeis University, Jerusalem's Martyrs Memorial Yad Vashem, the Israel Experience, and the National Foundation for Jewish Culture. He has also made considerable donations to the Cedars-Sinai Medical Center for pediatric medicine (they named a wing of the building after him), and is the Chairman Emeritus for the Starbright Foundation, which is dedicated to the development of projects that empower seriously ill children to combat the medical and emotional challenges they face. Via the Wunderkinder Foundation, he has donated to the American Heart Association, Children's Diabetes Foundation, Planned Parenthood of Los Angeles, Teddy Bear Cancer Foundation, and the UCLA Foundation towards medical research. *Tzedakah.*

Between 1979 and 2011, George Soros gave away over $8 billion to human rights, public health, and educational causes. He played a significant role in the peaceful transition from communism to capitalism in Hungary. Soros has been active as a philanthropist since the 1970s, when he began providing funds to help black students attend the University of Cape Town in apartheid South Africa, and began funding dissident movements behind the iron curtain. *Tzedakah.*

The first time a McDonald's franchise used the Golden Arches logo was in 1953. In 1955, Ray Kroc, joined the company as a franchise agent and quickly proceeded to purchase the chain from the McDonald brothers. Today, McDonald's is the world's largest restaurant chain by revenue, serving over 69 million customers daily in over 100 countries across approximately 36,900 locations. Joan Kroc, the widow of Ray Kroc, left $1.91 billion to ten organizations, including $1.5 billion to the Salvation Army and $200 million to National Public Radio. *Tzedakah.*

Veronica Atkins, the widow of Dr. Robert C. Atkins (of Atkins Diet fame), pledged her entire $500 million fortune to end "di-obesity" -- diabetes and obesity. Mrs. Atkins has emerged as a passionate advocate for children's health, working to eradicate childhood obesity and Type II diabetes. *Tzedakah.*

Microsoft co-founder Paul Allen grants $30 million every year to human services and health related organizations. His $100-million brain science institute (neuroscience and genomics-research programs) will help sort out neurological disorders. In 2014, the Allen Institute for Artificial Intelligence was created, its main focus to research and engineer artificial intelligence. He has also committed $100 million to the creation of the Allen Institute for Cell Science, whose mission is to investigate and create a virtual model of cells in the hope of bringing forth treatment of different diseases. To date, his charitable donations have exceeded $1 billion. *Tzedakah.*

Ronald Owen Perelman is one of the world's largest philanthropic donors. He established the Revlon/UCLA Women's Cancer Research Program for research into the causes and treatment of breast and ovarian cancer. He founded the Ronald O. Perelman Department of Dermatology at NYU Medical Center; provided significant support for such organizations as the National Breast Cancer Coalition Fund, Carnegie Hall, the Solomon R. Guggenheim Museum, Memorial Sloan-Kettering Hospital, and Mr. Perelman's alma mater, The University of Pennsylvania. He made a $50 million donation to the New York Presbyterian Hospital and Weill Cornell Medical Center to provide vital financial aid for Reproductive Medicine. He's additionally pledged $15 million to Stand Up to Cancer, a Pasadena, Calif., organization that supports cancer research and efforts to advance treatment for cancer patients; $5-million to the World Trade Center Memorial Fund, in New York; and $2.5 million to Ford's Theatre, in Washington, D.C. In August 2010, Mr. Perelman signed the Gates-Buffett Pledge, committing up to half his assets ($12 billion) to be designated for the benefit of charitable causes. *Tzedakah.*

Sumner Murray Redstone is the majority owner and Chairman of the Board of the National Amusements theater chain. Through National Amusements, Sumner Redstone and his family are majority owners of CBS Corporation, Viacom, MTV Networks, BET, and the film studio Paramount Pictures. Sumner Redstone announced a commitment of $105 million in charitable grants to fund research and patient care advancements in cancer and burn recovery at three major non-profit healthcare organizations. The cash contributions of $35 million each will be paid to FasterCures/The Center for Accelerating Medical Solutions, based in Washington D.C.; the Cedars-Sinai Prostate Cancer Center in Los Angeles, California; and the Massachusetts General Hospital in Boston, Massachusetts. Over the last few years, Redstone has contributed $2.1 million to the Global Poverty Project. He has contributed $500,000 (the largest donation the charity could accept) to the Cambodian Children's Fund, a nonprofit program that provides a wide range of critical health and educational services to impoverished and abused children in the capital city of Phnom Penh. In early 2010, Autism Speaks announced that Sumner Redstone made a $1 million donation to be applied to scientific research into autism's causes, improved treatments, and, ultimately, its cures. In July 2010, Redstone donated $24 million to the Keck School of Medicine of the University of Southern California to support cancer research. In September 2012, he donated $18 million to the Boston University School of Law, and an additional $10 million to the Harvard University School of Law. Since October 2012, Redstone has donated a total of $350,000 to the Go Campaign, which funds projects in 21 countries with a focus on helping orphans and other needy children. *Tzedakah.*

Bernard "Bernie" Marcus co-founded Home Depot and was the company's first CEO. He is an active philanthropist. Marcus contributed heavily to the launch of the Georgia Aquarium, which opened in downtown Atlanta. He also funded and founded The Marcus Institute, a center of excellence for the provision of comprehensive services for children and adolescents with developmental disabilities. In May 2005, Marcus was awarded the Others Award by the Salvation Army, its highest honor. He is currently chairman of the Marcus Foundation, whose focuses include children, medical research, free enterprise, Jewish causes, and the community. Marcus is on the Board of Directors and an active volunteer for the Shepherd Center, whose main focus is in providing care for war veterans with traumatic brain injuries. In 2012, Bernard Marcus was awarded the William E. Simon Prize for Philanthropic Leadership. *Tzedakah.*

Leonard Stern is the Chairman and CEO of the privately owned Hartz Mountain Industries. He was the founder and is the Chairman of Homes for the Homeless, which is the largest non-profit provider of residential, education and employment training centers in the United States, and since 1986, has served more than 630 homeless families and over 1,200 homeless children each and every day at five separate sites across New York City. He has also donated $30 million to NYU, his alma mater. *Tzedakah.*

Robert Meyerhoff, a Maryland real- estate developer, with his wife, developed an exceptional collection of post-World War II art worth $300 million that they have willed to the National Gallery of Art in Washington after his death. The Meyerhoffs have contributed widely to education, the most noteworthy of all is the Meyerhoff Scholars Program created in 1988 at the University of Maryland in Baltimore County funding science and math scholarships to black students. *Tzedakah.*

Mark Cuban, is the owner of Landmark Theatres, Magnolia Pictures, the National Basketball Association's Dallas Mavericks, and chairman of the HDTV cable network AXS TV. Mark Cuban started the Fallen Patriot Fund to help families of U.S. military persons killed or injured during the Iraq War, personally matching contributions with funds from the Mark Cuban Foundation. In June 2015 Cuban made a $5 million donation to Indiana University at Bloomington for the "Mark Cuban Center for Sports Media and Technology," which will be built inside Assembly Hall, the school's basketball arena. *Tzedakah.*

In 1987, Ronald S. Lauder, son of Estee Lauder, established the Ronald S. Lauder Foundation, a philanthropic organization that is dedicated to rebuild Jewish communities in Central and Eastern Europe. The foundation also supports student exchange programs between New York and various capitals in Central and Eastern Europe. Lauder is actively involved in numerous civic organizations, including the Conference of Presidents of Major American Jewish Organizations, the Jewish National Fund, the World Jewish Congress, the

American Jewish Joint Distribution Committee, the Anti-Defamation League, the Jewish Theological Seminary, Brandeis University, and the Abraham Fund. *Tzedakah.*

Sheldon Gary Adelson is the chairman and chief executive officer of the Las Vegas Sands Corporation, which operates The Venetian Resort Hotel Casino and the Sands Expo and Convention Center. He also owns the Israeli daily newspaper Israel HaYom. Adelson donated over $25 million to the Adelson Educational Campus in Las Vegas to build a high school. In 2006 Adelson contributed $25 million to the Yad Vashem Holocaust Martyrs' and Heroes' Remembrance Authority. Since 2007, the Adelson Family Foundation has made contributions totaling $200 million to Birthright Israel, which finances Jewish youth trips to Israel. He also donated $5 million to the Friends of the Israel Defense Forces in 2014. *Tzedakah.*

Michael and Susan Dell established the Michael and Susan Dell Foundation, which has provided $65 million in grants to three health-related organizations associated with the University of Texas: the Michael & Susan Dell Center for Advancement of Healthy Living, the Dell Pediatric Research Institute, and the Dell Children's Medical Center, as well as funding for a new computer science building at the University of Texas, Austin campus. The foundation has also committed more than $650 million to children's issues and community initiatives in the United States, India and South Africa. In 2014, he donated $1.8 million to the Friends of the Israel Defense Forces, and in 2017, in the wake of Hurricane

Harvey, Dell, a Houston native, pledged $36 million to relief efforts. *Tzedakah.*

Robert K. Kraft is the Chairman and Chief Executive Officer of The Kraft Group. His holdings include the National Football League's New England Patriots, and Gillette Stadium (where the Patriots play). The Kraft Group has donated over $100 million to a variety of philanthropic causes including education, child and women-related issues, healthcare, youth sports, and American and Israeli causes. In 2011, Robert and Susan Kraft pledged $20 million to Partners HealthCare to launch the Kraft Family National Center for Leadership and Training in Community Health, an initiative designed to improve access to quality healthcare at community health centers throughout New England. Among the many institutions the Krafts have supported are Columbia University, Harvard Business School, Brandeis University, College of the Holy Cross, Boston College, Tufts University, the Belmont Hill School, the Boys & Girls Clubs of Boston, and the Dana Farber Cancer Institute in Boston. In 2007, in recognition of a gift of $5 million in support of Columbia's intercollegiate athletics program, the playing field at Columbia's Lawrence A. Wien Stadium at the Baker Field Athletics Complex was named Robert K. Kraft Field. One of their most distinctive projects is supporting American Football Israel, including Kraft Family Stadium in Jerusalem and the Kraft Family Israel Football League. In 2017 Kraft announced a contribution of $6 million to build the first ever regulation size American football field in Israel. In June 2017, Robert Kraft, along with several NFL Hall of

Famers, traveled to Israel for the grand opening of the new Kraft Family Sports Campus. *Tzedakah.*

David Geffen is an American record executive, film producer, theatrical producer and philanthropist. In 1994, Geffen co-founded the DreamWorks SKG studio with Steven Spielberg and Jeffrey Katzenberg. David Geffen made a multiyear $300 million pledge to the UCLA School of Medicine. The grants reflected Geffen's primary interests in AIDS research and care, the arts, civil liberties and, following Sept. 11, substantial support to the families of firefighters and police officers killed in the World Trade Center terrorist attack. According to Forbes and other sources, Geffen has pledged to give whatever money he makes from now on to charity. *Tzedakah.*

Home builder and financial-services mogul Eli Broad and his wife Edythe have given $10 million to the Washington, D.C. Public Education Fund, $2.2 million to the Education Innovation Laboratory at Harvard, and $2 million to a Los Angeles charter-schools foundation. Lin Arison, the widow of the founder of Carnival Cruise Lines, sold a Monet and a Modigliani and put the proceeds of $39 million into her National Foundation for Advancement in the Arts. Raymond and Ruth Perelman donated $225 million to the Univ. of Pennsylvania Medical School. Mark Zuckerberg, the Facebook founder, pledged $100 million to the Newark, New Jersey school system. He has also signed the Giving Pledge giving away half his wealth (now valued at $74.2 billion) to philanthropic and charitable causes. William Ackman, the hedge-fund manager, has gifted $25 million to various causes including the Innocence Project and Centurion

Ministries, both of which work to free the wrongfully convicted. *Tzedakah. Tzedakah. Tzedakah.*

As noted, under the Giving Pledge, the wealthiest individuals and families agree to give more than half of their wealth to philanthropy or charitable causes during or after their lifetimes. Additional names accepting the Gates/Buffett Giving Pledge challenge, include Qualcomm co-founder Irwin Jacobs and his wife Joan; World Savings Bank founding director Bernard Osher and his wife, the Consul General of Sweden to San Francisco, Barbro Osher; media mogul Barry Diller (Expedia) and his wife, designer Diane von Furstenberg; Dan Gilbert, founder of Quicken Loans and owner of the Cleveland Cavaliers. Add Charles and Edgar Bronfman (Seagrams), Arthur Blank (Home Depot), Carl Icahn, and Jeffrey Skoll (e-Bay). Way to go, guys.
Tzedakah.

For three millennia, Jewish charitable giving has been both guided and defined by a series of basic principles and motivations. The philanthropist was guided by the biblical injunctions of "tzedakah," the pursuit of justice or righteousness, and "tikkun olam," the oft cited mandate to repair the world.

While many ethnic and religious groups are mainly focused on the afterlife and downplaying this world, Jews view wealth and success as a blessing and gift from God. Jews believe their role is to improve and perfect God's creations through work, creation, and innovation (I know, I've said it before, but it's worth repeating).

For Jews, wealth is a good thing, a worthy and respectable goal to strive toward. Judaism has never considered poverty a virtue. The first Jews were not poor, and that was good. The Jewish founding fathers, Abraham, Isaac and Jacob, were blessed with cattle and land in abundance. "With your financial house in order, it is easier to pursue your spiritual life." Having said that, let's get real....I've seen rich Jews, broke Jews, dumb Jews, smart Jews, Jews in debt, frugal Jews, ostentatious Jews, white collar crime Jews (think Bernie Madoff), and everything in between. We're just human like everybody else with all the same bad habits.

By the way, you know that elephant in the room that everyone feels so uncomfortable talking about...its name is..."TZEDAKAH"

A.S. Winston

MIRACLES HAPPEN TO THOSE WHO BELIEVE

How did Hebrew become the only dead language in history to be revived after 2,000 years? Why would millions of people from around the world leave their homes and move to a desert wasteland to build new lives for themselves? How did these people manage to turn a land more than 80% desert into one of the largest food and flower exporters in the world? Why have incredible achievements in science, medicine, and new technologies happened here in greater concentration than anywhere else? There are no logical answers. Some say these things can only be explained as miracles. Why argue?

Given the circumstances surrounding Israel's birth as a nation, and the odds against its survival, Israel should not exist as a nation today. Yet it not only exists, but seems to thrive in spite of its adversaries and in the face of circumstances that defy logic and reason. Israel's survival through the turbulent 20th century (and now into this century) has defied all reasonable logic.

If there are miracles, Israel itself has to be one. Born out of the ashes of the Holocaust, it was just one day old when it was attacked by twelve armies that the world fully expected would annihilate it. Israel didn't even have an army. And yet, Israel won.

Jewish culture is about family, education, and charity, all of which has contributed to our levels of high achievement.

Tel Aviv has become one of the world's foremost entrepreneurial hot spots. Israel has more high-tech start-ups per capita than any other nation on earth, by far. It leads the world in civilian research-and-development spending per capita. It ranks second behind the U.S. in the number of companies listed on the Nasdaq. Israel, with 7 million people, attracts as much venture capital as France and Germany combined.

Israel's technological success is the fruition of the Zionist dream. The country was not founded so stray settlers could sit among thousands of angry Palestinians in Hebron. It was founded so Jews would have a safe place to come together and create things for the world.

Some oil-rich states spend billions trying to build science centers. But places like Silicon Valley and Tel Aviv are created by a confluence of cultural forces, not money. Those surrounding nations do not have the tradition of free intellectual exchange and technical creativity. The result: between 1980 and 2000, Egyptians registered 77 patents. The Saudis registered 171. The Israelis registered 7,652. Once again, "Why the hell shouldn't we feel proud?" I believe in miracles. But I also believe in the success that hard work, effort, dedication, perseverance, and a strong belief in one's self, and one's goals can produce.

SAY IT LOUD, AND SAY IT PROUD!

THE WISDOM OF JEWISH CULTURE...

A proverb is a wise old saying -- a wise truth dressed up in literary language that is generally but not always true. Take the following with a grain of salt (and if you like, add some popcorn to it).

"A friend you have to buy; enemies you get for nothing."

"Against stupidity, God Himself is helpless."

"Don't ask questions of fairy tales."

"No matter how bad things get, you got to go on living, even if it kills you."

"When a father gives to his son, both laugh; when a son gives to his father, both cry."

"What you don't see with your eyes, don't witness with your mouth."

"What soap is for the body, tears are for the soul."

"Life is the biggest bargain. We get it for nothing."

"Only love gives us the taste of eternity."

"People make plans and God laughs."

"The poor fool is a man who falls on his back and breaks his nose."

"Rejoice not at thine enemy's fall – but don't rush to pick him up either."

"If not for fear, sin would be sweet."

"If the rich could hire the poor to die for them, the poor would make a very nice living."

"If charity costs nothing, the world would be full of philanthropists."

"A mother understands what a child does not say."

"Commit a sin twice and it will not seem a crime."

"God created one world full of small worlds."

"Don't look for more honor than your life merits."

"Worries go down better with soup than without."

"The sun will set today without your assistance."

"The longer a blind man lives, the more he sees."

"A coin in an empty barrel, makes a lot of noise."

"Do not be wise in words - be wise in deeds."

"Don't approach a goat from the front, a horse from the back, or a fool from any side."

"If God lived on earth, people would break his windows."

"Man drives, but the Creator holds the reins."

"Pray that you will never have to bear all that you are able to endure."

"When you have no choice, mobilize the spirit of courage."

"Ask not for a lighter burden, but for broader shoulders."

"Locks keep out only the honest."

"If one person calls you a donkey, ignore him; if two people call you a donkey, buy a saddle."

"You can't sit on two horses with one behind."

"With horses you check the teeth; with a human you check the brains."

"A bird that you set free may be caught again, but a word that escapes your lips will not return."

"A pessimist, confronted with two bad choices, chooses both."

"As you teach, you learn."

"Don't be sweet, lest you be eaten up; don't be bitter, lest you be spewed out."

"He that can't endure the bad, will not live to see the good."

"Not to have felt pain is not to have been human."

"The innkeeper loves a drunkard, but not for a son-in-law."

"The only truly dead are those who have been forgotten."

"When a habit begins to cost money, it's called a hobby."

"No one is as deaf as the man who will not listen."

"He who puts up with insult invites injury."

"Loose tongues are worse than wicked hands."

"Don't make a toil of pleasure."

"Don't live in a town where there are no doctors."

"Among those who stand, do not sit; among those who sit, do not stand. Among those who laugh, do not weep; among those who weep, do not laugh."

"When a thief kisses you, count your teeth."

"If the pupil is smart, the teacher gets the credit."

"Your health comes first--you can always hang yourself later."

"He who has children will never die of starvation."

"When one lives, one experiences."

"You can make the dream bigger than the night."

"Don't be scared when you have no other choice."

"The entire world rests on the tip of the tongue."

"Lovers and thieves always look for darkness."

"A clock that stands still is better than one that goes wrong."

"Even an angel cannot do two things at the same time."

"When the time comes for you to live, there aren't enough years."

"Mothers-in-law are fine so long as they are deaf and blind."

"A good friend is often better than a brother."

"If you don't want to do something, one excuse is as good as another."

"One old friend is better than two new ones."

"Even in heaven, it is not good to be alone."

"Charity covers a multitude of sins."

"Never waste good agony."

"If it must always be better, it can never be good enough."

"Cheap borsht is a blessing to the toothless."

"Truth is the safest lie."

The list is never-ending, but that's what 5778 years of generational wisdom and brunch at Grandma's brings you.

SAY IT! GO ON, SAY IT!

A.S. Winston

ALWAYS REMEMBER, GOLIATH WAS A 40 POINT FAVORITE OVER DAVID

Jews have stereotypically been considered people of the book rather than people of the jump shot, right cross, or home run. Eastern European Jews traditionally honored scholarship and learning over athletic prowess. Yet for many Jewish immigrants, and especially their children, participation in American sport during the first half of the 20th century became an important part of their pursuit of the American dream.

Sport has played an integral role in American Jewish identity. Jews used sports to strengthen ethnic pride, which helped ease their assimilation into American culture. Whether watching it or playing it, sports served as a middle ground between minority and majority cultures, between ethnic and racial minorities, and between generations of people who were actively determining for themselves what it meant to be American Jews. From settlement houses and street corners to Madison Square Garden, their experiences illuminated a time when Jewish males dominated sports (hard to believe, huh?).

Between World War I and World War II, Jewish athletes were the dominant ethnic group in professional boxing in the United States. Boxing was a means many second generation urban immigrants, including Jews, used to get ahead in the early 20th century. The Jewish boxers took up fighting to earn money, not to defend their race or to negate the stereotype that Jews were weak. These boxers were proud of their heritage and displayed Stars of David on their robes and trunks until religious symbols were banned in the 1940s. During the 1920s nearly one-third of all professional boxers were Jewish. They were the dominant ethnic group in the sport earning thirty World Championship titles between 1910 through 1940. Those were the days of the struggle for American Jews in the urban ghettos against poverty and anti-Semitism. Boxing was for many kids a way out.

On March 3, 1934, a group of young Jewish men helped change basketball history. On that night, fans in New York City watched with anticipation for the winner of a game between New York University (NYU) and City College of New York (CCNY).

The New York Times stated that the 20th annual meeting between the two schools had "never before aroused such widespread interest," as both teams entered the contest undefeated. The demand for tickets was such that promoters began a series of doubleheaders at Madison Square Garden the following season, and turned New York City into the center of the basketball world.

The next year Newsweek ran a story on basketball's rise to prominence and declared the sport was one "at which Jews excel."

Both the NYU-CCNY game (in which nine of the ten starters were Jewish), and the Newsweek article occurred during the peak of Jewish prominence in basketball. Yet, the story of Jewish basketball is more than either a single game or article. Centered in New York, Jews were crucial to the development of college and professional basketball during the first half of the 20th century. Invented by Dr. James Naismith at a YMCA in 1891, basketball quickly became a popular sport that expanded into the broader society.

The popularization of basketball amongst the Jewish youth in urban areas primarily occurred both in settlement houses and at communal institutions. The Jewish youth on New York's Lower East Side played basketball on playgrounds and at schoolyards. The formation of the Public School Athletic League (PSAL) in the early 1900s allowed players to gain experience in organized, competitive settings.

In the early 1920s, Jewish basketball spread throughout the country. As neighborhoods stabilized due to immigration restriction, American-born children began to embrace America's sporting culture. Jewish players often played at YMHAs, synagogues, and community centers before and after their college or professional careers. The rise of Jewish basketball reflected American Jews' larger story during the first half of the 20th century. From immigrant neighborhoods, Jews sought out opportunities to join the mainstream.

Success in basketball is just one story of achievement during a time of adjustment, stress, and occasional anti-Semitism. At the same time, Jews made a lasting contribution to the game. While few Jews played at the highest levels, the sport owes its development to its roots with those Jewish neighborhood teams.

100 years ago, we were the ones bouncing the basketball and stepping into the ring. But our destiny lay in another arena.

BELIEVE. ACHIEVE. SUCCEED.

In the movie "Airplane" when one of the passengers asks for light reading, they are given a pamphlet about Jewish sports stars. There we go being stereotyped once again…that American Jews and sports are somehow alien to each other, fueling the myth that the "Chosen People" are the last picked when anyone is choosing up sides.

Despite all that time spent with Torah, we also found time for Hank Greenberg and Sandy Koufax to be inducted into Baseball's Hall of Fame; Max Baer and Barney Ross were boxing champions; Allie Sherman and Marv Levy were NFL champion football coaches, while Sid Luckman and Sammy Baugh were two of the greatest quarterbacks to ever play the game; Mark Spitz won nine Olympic Gold Medals in swimming (also one Silver and one Bronze); Amy Alcott won five major golf championships; Mitch Gaylord was an Olympic Gold Medal winner in gymnastics; Harold Abrahams and Marty Glickman were track and field stars; Bill Goldberg (Goldberg) and Randy Travis were popular professional wrestlers; Mark Roth was four time professional bowler of the year; and Red Holtzman and Dolph Schayes are both NBA legacies.

And all that is nothing compared to what came next. Our "lantzmen" decided that when it came to the sporting world, ownership would be more fun, and profitable, than participation, and we were quickly knee deep in professional sports.

In baseball, we became owners of the Oakland Athletics, the New York Mets, the Pittsburgh Pirates, the Toronto Blue Jays, the Texas Rangers, the Washington Nationals, the Los Angeles Dodgers, the Baltimore Orioles, the Chicago White Sox, and the Tampa Bay Rays.

In the NFL, sports ownership continued with the Atlanta Falcons, the Oakland Raiders, the Tampa Bay Buccaneers, the New York Jets, the New England Patriots, the Cleveland Browns, the Philadelphia Eagles, the Atlanta Falcons, the St. Louis Rams, the Miami Dolphins, the Washington Redskins, the Minnesota Vikings, the Indianapolis Colts, the San Diego Chargers (who have since moved to Los Angeles), the Baltimore Ravens, and the New York Giants.

In the NBA, our entrepreneurial interests were extended with ownership of the Houston Rockets, the Miami Heat, the Dallas Mavericks, the Detroit Pistons, the Cleveland Cavaliers, the Milwaukee Bucks, the Brooklyn Nets, the Chicago Bulls, the Seattle Supersonics, the Toronto Raptors, the Portland Trail Blazers, the Boston Celtics, the Atlanta Hawks, the Philadelphia 76ers, the Golden State Warriors, the Washington Wizards, the Phoenix Suns, and the Los Angeles Clippers. And let's not forget Abe Saperstein, who founded (and owned) the Harlem Globetrotters.

The National Hockey League didn't escape our interests either, as we became owners of the Tampa Bay Lightning, the Boston Bruins, the Edmonton Oilers, the Anaheim Ducks, the New Jersey Devils, the New York

Islanders, the Nashville Predators, the Philadelphia Flyers, and the Toronto Maple Leafs.

Let's add our being commissioners of the National Basketball Association, Major League Baseball, Major League Soccer, and the National Hockey League. We've also served as Presidents and CEOs of the Chicago Cubs, the New York Yankees, the NFL Network, ABC Sports, Turner Sports (TBS, TNT), and the Madison Square Garden Corp.

It takes a sports agent to get you those lucrative TV endorsements. But that's only after they've gotten you a multi-million dollar contract. Take the highest paid athletes in sports and you will find the agents representing them are overwhelmingly Jewish.

You may not think of skiing as a kosher affair, but, the CEO of Vail Resorts (their holdings rooted in Colorado, include Vail, Beaver Creek, Breckenridge, and Keystone ski resorts) is Adam Aron. The CEO of American Skiing Company (Steamboat Springs in Colorado, Sunday River in Maine, Heavenly at Lake Tahoe, and the Canyons in Utah) is Les Otten, son of Jewish refugees from Nazi Germany. The Crown family owns the Aspen Ski Resort company.

Going to buy a hot dog at a sports event, thank Larry Levy, co-founder of Levy Restaurants. Want to study which horse to bet on in the big race? Moses Annenberg created the Daily Racing Form in 1922. The Sorin family founded and controls the famous Topps Baseball Card Co. Joe Gold founded Gold's Gym, and later World Gym. Joe Weider (weight training products) started the Mr. Olympia bodybuilding contest in the 1960s; he brought Arnold Schwartzenegger to America in 1968. Eric

Bischoff headed the World Champion Wrestling organization; the head of Brunswick, the billiards and bowling firm founded in the late 1800s, was John Brunswick (also Jewish).

The more you dig into the history of sports, the more you see the fingerprints of the Jewish people. We may have ended up in suits and ties, but we have definitely broken that stereotypical myth regarding that "alien relationship" with the wide, wide, world of sports.

Now here's a little something to nosh on...

Sandy Koufax was often referred to as "the left hand of God." No immortal in the history of baseball retired so young, so well, or so completely, as Sandy Koufax. After compiling a remarkable record from 1962 to 1966 that saw him lead the National League in ERA all five years, win three Cy Young awards, and pitch four no-hitters including a perfect game, Koufax essentially disappeared. Save for his induction into the Hall of Fame and occasional appearances at the Dodgers training camp, Koufax has remained unavailable, unassailable, and unsullied, in the process becoming much more than just the best pitcher of his generation. He is the Jewish boy from Brooklyn, who refused to pitch the opening game of the 1965 World Series on Yom Kippur, defining himself as a man who placed faith over fame.

When Ernest Hemingway wrote in 1932 that Latin America's only great American-born matador "is better, more scientific, more intelligent, and a more finished matador than all but six of the full matadors in Spain today, and the bullfighters know it and have the utmost respect for him," he was talking about Sidney Frumkin, a

Jew from Brooklyn, New York, who was affectionately called "El Torero de la Torah," the bullfighter of the Torah. Ole'.

The irony of Kerri Strug's moment of a lifetime is that it wasn't necessary. As it turned out, the final Russian faltered in her floor exercise, rendering Kerri Strug's second vault meaningless in the box score. Thankfully she didn't know it at the time, because what Kerri Strug did in Atlanta in 1996 is the most perfect example of the Olympic ideal, and it's why sport will forever be the ultimate reality show. The moment reads like a Hollywood script: USA vs. Russia, gold medal on the line, one team (the U.S.) about to choke away a lead with just one gymnast left, only she's just sprained her ankle. It was high drama being played out on live television in front of a worldwide audience: Kerri Strug standing at the foot of the runway on one good leg and one gimpy one, the gregarious Bela Karolyi urging her on, telling her she could do it even though no one knew if she could run, spring, and land, on that injured left ankle. And then, without hesitation, she was off. She ran, she sprang, she landed, then lifted her tender left ankle in the air as she turned on one leg to salute the judges. She'd done it – she'd clinched the United States' first Olympic gold medal ever in the women's team competition, and with room to spare. An entire nation kvelled. Kerri Strug conquered the world Olympic stage, and in so doing, became an icon that people will talk about forever.

Sports are an integral part of our American culture. They respond to deep human needs. They have contributed to racial and social integration. Social rituals have grown up around numerous athletic contests; from college tailgate parties, to baseball's World Series, to the planet's celebration of Super Bowl Sunday. No-one can deny the power of sports in American culture. Sports may not win elections, clean our streets, or lower gas prices. What they do is unite the most diverse country in the world. Race and religion don't matter. Culture and ethnicity don't matter. Sports provide a platform for people to come together. I know this sounds hokey, but one of the most positive things about sports is the pure, unadulterated joy it brings to everyone involved. Sports are emotional, and often incite great passion. Sometimes it's joyful, and other times, not so much. But anytime something can bring out that range of extreme, raw emotion in people, it's a good thing. You cannot deny the extent of our contributions, and our impact, on American society through sports. So, gather your own cheerleading squad, get your pom poms ready (or whatever), maybe add a little choreography, and SAY IT LOUD, AND SAY IT PROUD!

EVERYONE WAS NEEDED TO BUILD AMERICA, NOT JUST THE "RIGHT PEOPLE."

"I lived among trappers and Indians, but always as a Jew. Did I need grander temples to worship in? In the murmurs of the pines I hear the psalms of David: the fragrance of the incense is as of old, the winds speak to me in 'His Voice."

-From "The Sounding of the Shofar" – sermon, Rachel Frank 1892.

Contrary to popular thought, Jewish life in America was not exclusive to New York City and the east coast of America. Jews also made their homes throughout the West in locales as far flung as Waco, Texas; Spokane, Washington; Deadwood, South Dakota; and San Francisco, California.

Jewish trailblazers arrived in the West with the first Spanish expedition in the sixteenth century, trekked along the Santa Fe Trail in the 1820s with the Fremont expedition, and prospected for California gold in 1848. They ranged from the well-to-do to the very poor, and came from all over Europe (Germany, Poland, the Ukraine, and Russia). They became farmers, merchants, traders, educators, lawmakers, and leaders in the arts. Across the Great Plains and Texas hill country, in the arid

Great Basin, and along the lush Pacific Coast, they formed agricultural communities, changed the face of urban centers, and built schools, hospitals, and motion picture studios. Above all, they helped create a diverse Western community.

The New World was to the West. Instinctively from the time of Columbus the minds of men and women were drawn to the possibilities that existed in the West. It was from the West that new concepts of freedom, opportunity, equality, acceptance and toleration evolved as responses to the frontier. It was to the West, that the Jews were drawn seeking, finding, and securing, a level of freedom and acceptance unknown to them in Europe.

Peter Stuyvesant, the Governor of New Amsterdam attempted to expel the first permanent North American Jewish immigrants: 23 forlorn Jewish survivors from Recife, Brazil, who were cast upon the shores of New Amsterdam (New York) in September, 1654. The Jews were permitted to stay just so long as they did not become a burden, as long as they were self- reliant in the New World (our foot was in the door).We became self-reliant.

In time, we demanded and won the right to risk fate and fortune (and our lives), to immerse ourselves with our new identities as Americans. America was different. The Jew could become an American and be identified as such. Bigoted European ideas, imposing limits on how Jews could participate in America, were quickly abandoned; the demands of the frontier would not permit that. Everyone was needed to build America, not just the "right people."

Whether it was by wagon train or horseback, the frontier was pushed toward its manifest destiny, bounded only by the waters of the Atlantic in the East and the Pacific in the West. The movement west was neither a simple nor orderly process. It was an uncontrolled surging tide of humanity from all walks of life searching for opportunity and flowing wherever it could. They all came searching for "the golden ring" and a better life. And we were a part of that surging tide, realizing we could find a better, safer place in America.

The amazing thing for the European Jew in America was that he was permitted to be a part of it (America). The demands to open the frontier, to develop it, to defend it, to expand it, were not accepted reasons for denying the Jew a part in it. Prejudice did exist, but all men and women were needed.

On Sunday, March 6, 1836, the Alamo weakly defended by 183 Americans from twenty-three states and from five different countries under Col. William Travis and frontiersmen Jim Bowie and Davy Crockett, fell to the huge army of Mexican general Santa Ana. The surrendering defenders were brutally massacred. Among the dead were Avram Wolfe and his two young sons (ages 11 and 12). They were Jews who joined the fight for Texas freedom. It was not a freedom in name but a freedom in reality. Under Mexican law, Jews were not permitted freedom of religion; under Texas law they were free to worship and live openly as Jews. They fought for a freedom that was unknown to them in Europe. They fought and died not as Jews but as Americans.

John Sutter, high up in the remote Sierra Nevada Mountains of far off California, put his hand into the fast flowing, clear, cold mountain waters of the American

River. He planned to put up a saw mill. Instead he changed the world. Sutter found gold. From all over America, from all over Europe, from all over the world, the word "gold" rang out. It was not just gold, but also opportunity for all who were brave enough to reach for it. It was dangerous, and it would be deadly for some. White men, black men, Oriental men, Christian, Buddhist and Jew went to California to follow the "golden" opportunity. Some Jews were miners, but most were small businessmen and merchants. Some were doctors, some were lawyers. By 1870, 1/6th of San Francisco was estimated to be Jewish. By 1880 there were more Jews living in more small towns in California than in New York State.

How did we get there? Some rode "prairie schooners," the great Conestoga wagon trains across the "Great American desert" chancing Indian attack, thirst, fierce weather and worse. Some elected to go West around the dangerous Cape Horn, or across the disease laden Isthmus of Panama and up to California.

Jew helped Jew on the frontier. A Jewish merchant network developed, evolving from itinerate backpacking peddlers to store front merchants, eventually reaching from the frontier to New York to Europe.

Solomon Bibo arrived in the 1860's, joining his brothers and went to work in Santa Fe. He soon moved to Acoma, New Mexico, an Indian reservation south of Albuquerque. Bibo established a trading center that was respected for honesty and fair dealings by the Indians. Marriageable Jewish women were rare on the frontier. Most of the immigrants were single, young Jewish men. If a man wanted a wife he would have to send for a match to the East (New York), or even further East (Europe). For many Jewish men, including Solomon Bibo, this was not realistic. He married a woman from the Acoma Indian tribe. Her name was Juanna. Unlike some tribes, the Acoma Indians elected their tribal chiefs to represent their interests against the encroachments of the outside world. They chose whom they felt would do the best for them. The Acoma Indians elected Solomon Bibo to be their Governor, to be their Chief, in 1885. It was an extraordinary choice. A man who spoke Yiddish, Spanish, and Queres (the Acoma Indian language). A man who had studied Talmud and Torah stood on the Acoma Pueblo Mesa and looked out over the Indian lands of the Acoma people, had become an American Indian Chief.

Josephine Marcus was born in 1861 in New York. Her family moved to San Francisco where the young independent, headstrong girl grew up with a spirit of adventure. She ran off to perform on the stage and found herself working in a saloon in Tombstone, Arizona. Josephine Marcus was a vivacious dark haired and fiery eyed daughter of Israel, working for the local sheriff. The sheriff ran the saloons, the whore houses and the girls. His name was Wyatt Earp. Earp fell for the young Jewess, and she for him. Together their lives would be shaped by a gunfight between the Earp Brothers, Doc Holiday and the Clantons. The gunfight went down in American history and Western lore as the "Gunfight at the O.K. Corral." Wyatt Earp and Josephine Marcus were joined, some say by marriage others by simply love, for the next fifty years. They are buried side by side in the Jewish Cemetery, Little Hills of Eternity, in Colma, California, not far from Solomon and Juana Bibo.

The freedom that the movement west offered did not guarantee success. It offered opportunity, toleration and acceptance. On the developing frontier, these new American Jews acquired new skills as merchants, bankers, freighters, miners, town-builders, ranchers, farmers, teachers, lawyers, doctors, and officeholders. American Jews in the west became pioneers, frontiersman, Indian fighters, Indians, ranchers, gunfighters, even creators of the great American Wild West shows. Jews were Mayors and sheriffs, from San Francisco, California, to Deadwood, South Dakota, where today their bones rest in cemeteries like "Hebrew Hill." Jews were elected State Governors in Idaho and Utah, before a Jew was ever elected as a Governor in the East.

In sprouting cities and small towns, they established Jewish benevolent societies, burial grounds, synagogues, and temples. Wealthy, middle-class, poor, traditionalist, reformer, and renegade, they all helped transform the new American West, and in the process, were themselves transformed.

THE GRAND PRIZE WAS LIFE

"Reality TV" is a genre of television programming that presents, allegedly, unscripted dramatic, or humorous situations, and usually features "ordinary" people instead of professional actors, in a contest or other situation where a prize is awarded. I'm not a big fan of reality TV. But imagine a reality TV show based on history, the purest form of reality. You can't change history, nor should it ever be forgotten. Imagine the show "Survivor" being played out, not on some scenic remote island, but instead at Auschwitz, under WWII conditions. Now that's reality TV, with the grand prize being… LIFE.

Some memories are painful, yet they are part of the fabric of who we are. And no one should ever forget that "once upon a time" madness ruled our world, and everyone got a close-up look at evil. 6 million Jews, 20 million Russians, 10 million Christians, 1,900 Catholic priests, murdered, massacred, raped, burned, starved and humiliated. 130,000-500,000 Gypsies; 150,000-200,000 handicapped persons; approx. 10,000 gay men; about 1,000 Jehovah's witnesses. The fate of black people from 1933 to 1945 in Nazi Germany and in German-occupied territories ranged from isolation to persecution, sterilization, medical experimentation, incarceration, brutality, and murder. World War II was not a myth. The programs of genocide were not a myth. The Holocaust is not the private nightmares of just the Jews. Spread the word…

NEVER FORGET…

"I marvel at the resilience of the Jewish people. Their best characteristic is their desire to remember. No other people has such an obsession with memory."

--Elie Wiesel

Zinovii Tolkachev was a Jewish soldier in a Russian Army unit that participated in the liberation of the notorious death camp, Auschwitz, in 1945. Horrified by the nightmare scenes that greeted him, two images forever etched themselves into his memory. The first was the tortured faces of the cold, malnourished children who were to be the next victims of the "Final Solution." And the second image that would haunt him was the mountain of tiny shoes stripped from countless Jewish boys and girls whose short lives would end in a cloud of poison gas.

To commemorate the victims, Tolkachev reached into the mountain of footwear and randomly selected a small black leather shoe to keep as a lifelong reminder of these darkest of days.

To preserve the images of the living, Tolkachev furiously sketched the faces of the children on the back of blank forms commandeered from camp headquarters. These were later published in a book entitled *Flowers of Auschwitz,* which Tolkachev dedicated "For all of the children in the world, so they may never be forgotten."

Some 53 years later, both the sketches and the shoe had taken separate paths to a place where their stories are told. That place is Yad Vashem, the first and foremost memorial erected by the Jewish people to the victims of the *Shoah*, the final resting place for six million Jews, on the Mount of Remembrance in Jerusalem.

Six million Jewish lives lost. Six million individuals wiped off the face of the earth. Yet each one of them was a thinking, feeling person, precious and unique.

NEVER FORGET!

In the talented hands of a 12-year-old Jewish boy from Belorussia, his violin sang so sweetly that he was required to play twice a day, at lunch and dinner, in a German officer's mess. Motteleh, as the boy was called, received food and could have remained content for some time. But the murder of his entire family in the early days of the war weighed heavily on him, and he was consumed with avenging their deaths.

In time, he developed a plan. Each night after his meal, he hid his precious violin in the cellar of the mess and left with an empty case. Each day when he returned, he smuggled into the building the explosives he hid inside the now heavily loaded case.

On the day the officers of an SS Division stopped to dine, Motteleh tiptoed into the cellar, lit a fuse attached to nearly 40 pounds of explosives, and escaped into the night, this time accompanied by a deafening explosion and the sounds of shattering glass. Motteleh did not survive the war.

But Motteleh's violin, and his story live on.

The world's foremost Holocaust memorial provides a home for these priceless reminders, to tell their story again and again, for every succeeding generation to NEVER FORGET!

A plain, rusted bicycle, with a bell that still rings, was used in 1942 as part of a last ditch effort to save as many French Jews as possible from deportation to the German death camps. When the local Bishop drafted a pastoral letter condemning the mass expulsion, he requested the assistance of Marie-Rose Gineste in delivering the proclamation to all forty churches in the region in time to be read at the next Sunday Mass.

Fearing authorities might censor the letter if mailed, Marie-Rose decided to deliver it in person. And so she spent the next two days on the bicycle peddling from parish to parish and ensuring the condemnation was read in every church in the diocese. The effect was that many French families hid Jews or prevented them from being deported as a result of the message.

Since the end of the war, she kept the bicycle to remind her of that fateful journey. And now, she's made it her wish that the bicycle be taken to Yad Vashem, to serve as a reminder for future generations of the courage needed to take a stand for what is right.

NEVER FORGET a small child's black leather shoe, a well-played violin, an old rusty bicycle, and the millions of Jews who were forever lost, and the survivors who would be forever changed. NEVER FORGET!

Mrs. Clare Booth-Luce, the wife of Henry Luce, the founder of TIME magazine, was a well-respected and highly-informed writer and journalist. It must have been in the late '60's that she said, at a gathering of academics and politicians, to a prominent Jewish leader (Nachum Goldman), "I really feel that the Jews should stop commemorating the Holocaust. Why don't you get on with life, put all those experiences, however painful they may be, behind you and concentrate on the future?"

Nachum Goldman stood silent for a moment; then, with brightly shining eyes and a warm smile on his face, he said, "Mrs. Luce, those are exactly my sentiments when I hear people talk about the Crucifixion."

"I've gotta tell ya' mister, that's an awfully boring tattoo on your arm. It's just a bunch of numbers."

"Well, I was about your age when I got it, and kept is as a reminder."

"Oh, a reminder of happier days?"

"No...of a time when the world went mad. Imagine yourself in a land you called home, where your countrymen suddenly started following the voices of political extremists, who didn't like you simply because of your religion. Imagine having everything taken from you. Your entire family sent away to a concentration camp as slave laborers, then systematically murdered. A place where they take your name and replace it with a number tattooed on your arm. It was a time of madness called the holocaust, when millions of people perished just because of their faith."

"So you keep it to remind yourself of the dangers of political extremism?"

"No, dear boy, to remind you."

SAY IT LOUD AND SAY IT PROUD! AND NEVER FORGET!

THE CHALLENGES OF STATEHOOD

Antisemitism may be manifested in many ways, ranging from expressions of hatred of or discrimination against individual Jews, to organized violent attacks by mobs, state police, or even military attacks on entire Jewish communities. Notable instances of Jewish persecution include the pogroms which preceded the First Crusade in 1096, the expulsion from England in 1290, the massacres of Spanish Jews in 1391, the persecutions of the Spanish Inquisition, the expulsion from Spain in 1492, Cossack massacres in the Ukraine, various pogroms in Russia, the Dreyfus affair, the Holocaust, official Soviet anti-Jewish policies, and the Jewish exodus from Arab and Muslim countries.

The post Holocaust history of Israel saw her officially recognized as a state with her own democratic government in 1948. One year after World War II, 250,000 Holocaust survivors made their way to Israel. The Arab countries surrounding the small state made a pact between themselves not to recognize, negotiate, or make peace with Israel. But they didn't stop there. The wars launched against the new state were the Arab-Israeli war, the Suez war with Egypt, the creation of the P.L.O., the Six-Day war, the Yom Kippur War, the Lebanon war, Intifadas, the attacks on Israel by Saddam Hussein from Iraq with scud missiles in 1990-1991, and the Gaza conflict in 2005. In reality, not a day goes by that Israel isn't in conflict with its neighbors.

For Israel, nothing has come easily or for free. No U.N. declaration can create a new nation. At Jerusalem's military cemetery, prime ministers and ordinary soldiers are buried in adjacent sections. Simple gravestones tell the stories of young people who survived Hitler's ovens, only to give their lives in Israel's war for independence. The Jewish state's borders have changed since statehood as a result of subsequent wars. Yet Israel remains the only nation in history to bargain for peace by voluntarily giving up land (in 1982 Israel returned the Sinai, gained during the Six Day War, to Egypt in return for the peace treaty in effect today).

Since Israel saw statehood, her intelligence network became the best and most accurate in the world. Israeli teams rescued hostages taken in Entebbe, Uganda. They rescued their people from oppressive nations like Ethiopia, as seen in "Operation Elijah," "Operation Moses," and "Operation Solomon" in 1991, when Israel airlifted the remainder of Ethiopian Jewry to safety.

There is a famous story in which the Kaiser asks Bismarck, "Can you prove the existence of God?" Bismarck replies, "The Jews, your majesty. The Jews."

SOMETIMES, EVEN TO LIVE, IS AN ACT OF COURAGE

For around $500.00 you can purchase a wedding dress at a larger retailer that is machine made. Brides who are looking for a designer wedding dress in silk, or other natural fabric, should expect to pay between $2,000 and $4000. For brides who have an extravagant budget, expect to pay $6,000.00 and up for a designer wedding dress custom made just for you. Vera Wang designed wedding dresses have been known to cost $25,000 and more. Grace Kelly's wedding dress cost $65,000. Kate Middleton's wedding dress cost $400,000. Princess Diana's wedding dress is priceless. And then there's Lilly Friedman.

Lilly Friedman doesn't remember the last name of the woman who designed and sewed the wedding gown she wore when she walked down the aisle more than sixty years ago. But the grandmother of seven does recall that when she first told her fiancé Ludwig that she had always dreamed of being married in a white gown, he realized he had his work cut out for him.

For the tall, lanky twenty-one year-old who had survived hunger, disease and torture, this was a different kind of challenge. How was he ever going to find such a dress in Bergen-Belsen's displaced person's camp, where they felt grateful just to have the clothes on their backs?

Fate would intervene in the guise of a former German pilot who walked into the food distribution center where Ludwig worked, eager to make a trade for his worthless parachute. In exchange for two pounds of coffee beans and a couple of packs of cigarettes, Lilly Friedman would have her wedding gown.

For two weeks Miriam the seamstress worked under the curious eyes of her fellow DPs, carefully fashioning the six parachute panels into a simple, long-sleeved gown with a rolled collar and a fitted waist that tied in the back with a bow. When the dress was completed she sewed the leftover material into a matching shirt for the groom.

A white wedding gown may have seemed like a frivolous request in the surreal environment of the camps, but for Lilly Friedman the dress symbolized the innocent, normal life she and her family had once led before the world descended into madness. Lilly Friedman and her siblings were raised in a Torah-observant home in the small town of Zarica, Czechoslovakia, where her father was a teacher, respected and well-liked by the young yeshiva students he taught. He and his two sons were marked for extermination immediately upon arriving at Auschwitz. For Lilly and her sisters it was only their first stop on their long journey of persecution, which included Plashof, Neustadt, Gross-Rosen, and finally Bergen-Belsen.

Four hundred people marched fifteen miles in the snow to the town of Celle on January 27, 1946, to attend Lilly and Ludwig's wedding. The town synagogue, damaged and desecrated, had been lovingly renovated by the DPs with the meager materials available to them. When a Torah arrived from England, they converted an old kitchen cabinet into a makeshift Aron Kodesh, or Holy Ark.

Six months later, Lilly Friedman's gown was in great demand. Her sister Ilona wore the dress when she married. After that came her cousin Rosie. How many brides wore Lilly Friedman's dress? "I stopped counting after 17," she said. With the camps experiencing the highest marriage rate in the world, Lilly's gown was in great demand.

When President Harry Truman finally permitted the 100,000 Jews who had been languishing in DP camps since the end of the war to emigrate in 1948, the gown accompanied Lilly Friedman across the ocean to America. Unable to part with her dress, it lay at the bottom of her bedroom closet for the next 50 years, "not even good enough for a garage sale. I was happy when it found such a wonderful home."

Home was the U.S. Holocaust Memorial Museum in Washington, D.C. When Lilly Friedman's niece, a volunteer, told museum officials about her aunt's dress, they immediately recognized its historical significance and displayed the gown in a specially designed showcase, guaranteed to preserve it for 500 years.

But Lilly's dress had one more journey to make — the Bergen-Belsen museum, which opened on Oct. 28, 2007. The German government invited Lilly and her sisters to be their guests for the grand opening. Although they initially declined the invitation, the family finally traveled to Hanover the following year with their children, their grandchildren and extended families to view the extraordinary exhibit created for the wedding dress made from a parachute.

Lilly Friedman's family, who were all familiar with the stories about the wedding in Celle, were eager to visit the synagogue. They found the building had been completely renovated and modernized. But when they pulled aside the handsome curtain they were astounded to find that the Aron Kodesh, made from a kitchen cabinet, had remained untouched as a testament to the profound faith of the survivors. As Lilly Friedman stood on the bimah once again, she beckoned to her granddaughter, Jackie, to stand beside her where she was once a bride.

"It was an emotional trip. We cried a lot," she said.

Two weeks later, the woman who had once stood trembling before the selective eyes of the infamous Dr. Josef Mengele returned home and witnessed the marriage of her granddaughter.

The three Friedman sisters, Lilly, Ilona and Eva, who together survived Auschwitz, a forced labor camp, a death march and Bergen-Belsen, have remained close and today live within walking distance of each other in Brooklyn, New York. As mere teenagers they managed to outwit and outlive a monstrous killing machine, then went on to marry, have children, grandchildren and great grandchildren and were ultimately honored by the country that had earmarked them for extinction.

As young brides, they had stood underneath the chuppah and recited the blessings that their ancestors had been saying for thousands of years. In doing so, they chose to honor the legacy of those who had perished by choosing life.

NOT BAD FOR TWO POUNDS OF COFFEE BEANS AND A COUPLE OF PACKS OF CIGARETTES.

"JESUS WAS A JEW, YES, BUT ONLY ON HIS MOTHER'S SIDE." - Archie Bunker

When 23 Jews arrived on these shores from Recife, Brazil in 1654, Governor Peter Stuyvesant immediately wrote to his Dutch West India Company bosses requesting permission to ship back to their point of origin these "members of a deceitful race" who threatened to "infect and trouble this new colony."

But why did Stuyvesant, who had in fact allowed other Jewish immigrants to remain, sound the alarm bell with this group? Among this new set of immigrants, for the first time, were Jewish women. The few Jewish traders who had come earlier were apt to take non-Jewish wives for lack of their own kind; sooner or later, these men would disappear altogether as an ethnic entity. But the arrival of Jewish women meant families, nesting, and community, which would in turn enable other Jews to follow. The presence of Jewish women in 1654 signaled that Jews were here to stay.

And stay they did. From that handful of immigrant women, we have flourished to this day, when a Jewish woman sits on the Supreme Court, serves as governor of a state, owns a Forbes 400 company, wins the Nobel Prize in medicine, and presides over an Ivy League college; when Jewish women create and head national Jewish organizations, serve as rabbis and cantors of major

American synagogues, distinguish themselves in the two houses of Congress, and as mayors of major American cities; reach the pinnacle as leaders in fashion, literature and the arts; achieve fame in sports; and a time when an Orthodox woman has stood with public pride for many months while helping her husband run for an office (vice-president of the United States) infinitely higher than governor of New York. In three and a half centuries, we have come a very long way. Not only is it one of the most glorious chapters of Jewish history, but the work of Jewish women has richly enhanced American life in every imaginable arena.

Sabra is the term used for a native-born Israeli. The allusion is to a tenacious, thorny desert plant, known in English as Prickly Pear, with a thick skin that conceals a sweet, softer interior. The cactus is compared to Israelis, who are supposedly tough on the outside but delicate and sweet on the inside. In 2017, 75% of Israel's population (8,680,000) were sabras.

"I solemnly swear…to devote all of my strength and to sacrifice my life to protect the land and the liberty of Israel," says the newly recruited eighteen year old soldier during her swearing-in ceremony. She will enter a two-year period in which she will change from teenager to woman, dedicating her life to her country, all under a militaristic environment, and in the confines of an army that is engaged in daily war and conflict.

Israel is the only country in the world with a mandatory military service requirement for women. Women have taken part in Israel's military (Israeli Defense Forces a/k/a IDF) before and since the founding of the state in 1948, with women currently comprising

33% of all IDF soldiers and 51% of its officers, fulfilling various roles within the Ground, Navy, and Air Forces.

Female conscription is the law in Israel. Everyone serves. The desire to serve is as strong among the girls as it is among the boys. From their mid-teen years they live the military culture and want to serve their country and contribute to its safety and well-being.

Women serve in support and combat support roles in the IDF, but they do not serve in active combat. Around the world there has been discussion about whether or not women should serve in active front-line combat. In Israel it is clear that despite the vast contribution of women in the military, active combat is not an option. This decision is based on the physical and biological differences between men and women, and also for moral reasons. As a combat fitness instructor in the IDF once said, "No one wants to even think of the possibility of an Israeli girl falling into the hands of the enemy. Our history is already filled with too many such stories of atrocities."

Women serve in many capacities in the IDF, such as intelligence, the Border Police, maintenance, supplies, secretarial duties, as well as serving in a variety of technical and administrative support roles. Women can also be found servicing IDF computerized systems, working as computer programmers, smart weapons systems operators, and electronics technicians. Women have long served in technological positions, intelligence, operations, and training.

Over the course of the years, the number of military occupational specialties open to women in the IDF has expanded and today the Israeli woman is limited by nothing but her own ability.

These are strong women in character and skills, who have guns and know how to use them. Now there's a chilling combination. ARMED PRICKLY PEARS!!!

EVERYBODY ENJOYS KVELLING

Kvelling is something that ranges from casual to a high art form. In this age of social media, we all know how that goes. From the people who document every wondrous move their children make starting with breathing, to the humble-braggers that moan about their shin splints from running their third marathon this year. Kvelling may be of Jewish origin, but it is not ours exclusively. While many people believe it is part of our DNA, that doesn't mean the rest of the world cannot share the feeling, or express themselves in the same way.

An entire nation of African-Americans kvelled when Barack Obama became the first African-American President of the United States.

Just mention the name Frank Sinatra and listen to Italians proudly kvell (and rightly so), about one of the greatest voices of all time.

When Sandra Day O'Connor became the first female member of the Supreme Court of the United States, women everywhere kvelled, saying "it's about time."

Bruce Lee was probably the greatest martial artist of all time, and Asians throughout the world celebrated his talents.

Billy Crystal must have kvelled, when, in 1991, the Anti-Defamation League named him the entertainer of the year, and gave him an original seat from Yankee Stadium.

Kvelling has no ethnic or religious boundaries. Despite its origin, its meaning is universal. Everybody enjoys kvelling.

Four Catholic ladies were having coffee. The first Catholic woman tells her friends "My son is a priest. When he walks into a room, everyone calls him "Father."

The second Catholic woman chirps, "My son is a bishop. Whenever he walks into a room, people call him, "Your Grace."

The third Catholic mother says, "My son is a cardinal. Whenever he walks into a room, people say, "Your Eminence."

Since the fourth Catholic woman sips her coffee in silence, the first three women give her this subtle, "Well?"

So she replies, "My son is a gorgeous, 6' 2", hard-bodied dancer. When he walks into a room, people say, "Oh my God!"

We kvell about a new car, or our college alma mater. We kvell about how much weight we lost, or having given up smoking. We kvell about being accepted to medical school, and watching our baby take his (or her) first steps, or say his (or her) first words. And yes we kvell about our incredibly talented children (the doctor, lawyer, and Indian chief), and grandchildren (where there are no limits to kvelling).

Leah meets her old friend Naomi and they start talking about their families.

"So how's your son getting on?" Leah asks.

"Oy," replies Naomi, kvelling, "what nachas my Sheldon gives me. He's a doctor, you know, and he just

opened a big office in the city. His patients all work for the top banks and brokers and insurance companies. And he's a very good doctor, Leah; you should go see him for a checkup."

"Listen, Naomi" Leah replies. "I'm in perfect health. Nothing's wrong. So who needs a checkup?"

"I wouldn't be too confident about that, Leah," Naomi says. "If you go see my Sheldon, I promise you he will find something wrong."

And when it comes to sports, boy do we kvell. The Chicago Cubs winning the World Series for the first time in 108 years, and the city of Chicago erupts in a "kvellabration; the Pittsburgh Steelers winning the Super Bowl for the sixth time, and the kingdom of Pittsburgh reigns; the Los Angeles Lakers winning the NBA Championship for the sixteenth time, and Kobeland replaces Neverland. Who won the BCS college football championship? Who stood tall at the end of March Madness? How many gold medals did we take home from the Olympics?

Kvelling is good. It's healthy. When good things happen in our universe, we want to share. It is not boasting. It is not a sense of superiority. It's a feeling of satisfaction and achievement we are connected to emotionally, that somehow makes us feel good about ourselves, that provides the urge to share some of this satisfaction with others, and hope that they too will feel that sense of pride and accomplishment with you. These are all feelings that any of us can identify with and probably have acted on. Kvelling…share the joy.

Sadie is out shopping at Bloomingdale's, when she bumps into Becky, an old friend of hers. Becky is looking after her two grandchildren while their mother does some shopping on her own. Sadie says, "Oh Becky, what beautiful children. How old are they?"

Becky kvelled, "Well, the lawyer is six months, and the doctor is two years."

When Richard Dreyfuss was presented an award on behalf of Tel Aviv's Museum of the Jewish Diaspora by Consul General Uri Savir, Dreyfuss said the award was more important to him than the Oscar. "The Oscar you get for playing someone else. This award you get for being yourself. For the Oscar, you have a long list of people to thank. For this, you thank only your mother." Imagine how his mother felt.

Kvelling, just one more small contribution to mankind. And, under the best of circumstances, highly contagious.

SAY IT LOUD, AND SAY IT PROUD!

AND THEN THERE'S CHUTZPAH

If you grew up Jewish and American in a certain time and place, Yiddish, that linguistic mishmash of German, Hebrew, drama and high sarcasm, was always in the background, if not at the forefront, of your everyday life. As a young boy, I felt that Yiddish was the official "language of secrets" in my family. Whenever there was a family get-together, or a phone conversation when the relatives of my parents' generation wanted to say something that they did not want us kids to understand, they always spoke in Yiddish. Yiddish expressions. Yiddish phrases. It was particularly frustrating, because it seemed that every time someone said something in Yiddish, it was almost always answered with lots and lots of laughter, or a series of rapid-fire enthusiastic responses, or worse, both. Not only were we left out of the conversation, but it was always something that was really funny and unanimously approved of (this unanimity in a large Jewish family gathering was pretty rare in itself). Then the thought occurred to us children, grandchildren and cousins; maybe all these funny things they were saying were about us. Maybe they were making fun of us, and we were completely unable to know what it was they were saying. And of course, the more we asked what they were talking about, the more they looked to each other and continued to speak in this mysterious language, and continued to laugh. Yiddish is probably the most expressive language in the world. Face it, how can you be saying something good by saying a word that you practically have to spit in order to pronounce properly?

Many English words of Yiddush origin have entered the English language by way of American English. The Yiddish language is a wonderful source of rich expressions, especially terms of endearment (and of course, complaints and insults). You might be surprised to learn how much Yiddish you already speak.

NACHES: Jewish children are expected to provide their parent with naches (joy) till they graduate from medical school. And that's just for openers.

CHAZEREI: French fries, potato chips, sodas, cinema popcorn, twinkies, donuts, cookies, candy, pizza, in other words, everything from all the fun food groups that's no good for you.

A BI GEZUNT: "Don't worry so much about a problem, whatever it is. You've still got your health."

SHALOM: It means "deep peace," and isn't that a more meaningful greeting than "Hi, how are ya?"

SHLEP: To drag, traditionally something you don't really need (and definitely not one of the Three Stooges)

SCHLEMIEL: A clumsy, inept person, similar to a klutz (also a Yiddish word). The kind of person who always spills his soup.

SHMENDRIK: This means that the person is a jerk, but much bigger than a normal jerk. He is the master of all jerks.

SHMOOZE: A tradition for all who enjoy talking about nothing in particular.

TSUTCHEPPENISH: Yeah, this one doesn't spill from my lips too often. I can't spell it so I can never look it up, but it means something irritating that attaches itself like an obsession (I know a few people like that).

SCHMUCK: Needs no explanation.

SHIKSE: A non-Jewish woman.

SHMUTZ: a little dirt.

SHTICK: Something you're known for doing, a gimmick often done to draw attention to yourself.

TCHATCHKE: Knick-knack, little toy, collectible or giftware (a/k/a dust collector).

TSURIS: Serious troubles, not minor annoyances. Plagues of lice, gnats, flies, locusts, hail, volcanic eruptions, death… now, there was tsuris.

TUCHES: Rear end, bottom, backside, buttocks, and was the origin of the American slang word 'tush.' The New York Times called it an "insufficiently elegant" word.

YENTA: a busybody; a gossip; a walking, talking National Enquirer.

ZOFTIG: Marilyn Monroe and Anna Nicole Smith were zoftig. Audrey Hepburn and Callista Flockhardt were/are decidedly not zoftig.

BISSEL: A little bit (not the vacuum cleaner).

KOCKAMAYME: ridiculous, silly, crazy. "Afghanistan for vacation!? You and your kockamayme ideas!"

SCHMOE: This means a stupid or naive person (and again, not one of the Three Stooges)

SHTUPPING: (here again, needs no explanation)

FARSHTAIST? Understand? You got that? You dig, man? Comprende'? Capisce?

PULKES: Thighs. Please note: this word has been traced back to the language of one of the original Tribes of Israel, the Cellulites.

NEBISH: A nothing, a nobody. Woody Allen, the early years.

SHLIMAZEL: the guy with the rain cloud always over his head; when the shlemiel spills his soup, it's the shlimazel he spills it on.

UNGEHSHTUPPED: stuffed with money, loaded (a giant shtup would not be the correct definition).

SHMEKELEH: An inconsequential shmuck.

FARSHIKKERT: drunk as a skunk, three sheets to the wind.

FARFUFKET: Disoriented, befuddled (I just like the sound of this word).

OYSGEMITCHET: Exhausted (another word I like the sound of).

BUBBE: It means Grandmother, Nana, love.

BUPKES: Trivial, worthless, useless, a ridiculously small amount – less than nothing, so to speak.

FEH: An expression of disgust or disapproval.

GLITCH: common American usage as "a minor problem or error," except when it happens in space.

KLUTZ: Literally means "a block of wood," so it's often used for a dense, clumsy or awkward person, a/k/a schlemiel.

KOSHER: Something that's acceptable to Orthodox Jews, especially food. In English, when you hear something that seems suspicious or shady, you might say, "That doesn't sound kosher."

KVETCH: To complain, whine or fret…a true Jewish pastime.

MAVEN: An expert, one who knows it all; often used sarcastically.

MAZEL TOV: a congratulation for what just happened,

MENTSH: An honorable, decent person, an authentic person, a person who helps you when you need help.

MISHEGAS: Insanity or craziness (inviting the entire family for the holidays is mishegas)

SCHMALTZ: Chicken fat...the prime ingredient in almost every Jewish dish for the last five millennia.

MISHPOCHEH: It means "family."

NOSH: To nibble; a light snack (you can nosh on a bagel, you can't nosh on a prime rib).

NU: A general word that calls for a reply. It can mean, "So?" "Huh?" "Well?" "What's up?" "Hello?" How are things? How about it? What can one do? I dare you!"

OY VEY: The quintessential expression for that moment when you miss the train, spill red wine on your white tablecloth, or simply can't hear another word from your mother-in-law.

PLOTZ: To collapse or faint, as from surprise, excitement, or exhaustion. "You're not smoking that filthy thing in here. I'll plotz,"

And just for fun, let's add…

JEWBILATION: Pride in finding out that one's favorite celebrity is Jewish

SCHMUCKLUCK: Finding out one's wife became pregnant after one had a vasectomy.

……and then there's 'CHUTZPAH'

A little old lady sold pretzels on a street corner for 25 cents each. Every day a young man would leave his office building at lunch time, and as he passed the pretzel stand, he would leave her a quarter, but never take a pretzel. This went on for more than a year. The two of them never spoke. One day, as the young man passed the old lady's stand and left his quarter as usual, the pretzel lady spoke to him. Without blinking an eye she said, "They're 35 cents now." (that, ladies and gentlemen, is CHUTZPAH!).

TORAH…TORAH…TORAH…

If all of Judaism could be summarized in one word, that word would be God. When people around the world were worshiping thunder and wind, the Jews had but one word to say – 'God.' When people were lionizing the Spartan and the gladiator, the Jews had but one word to say - 'God.' And when, in every age, people searched for meaning, sanctity, and spirituality, the Jews had but one word to say - 'God.'

"They were the first people to arrive at an abstract notion of God and to forbid his representation by images. No people has produced a greater historical impact from such comparatively insignificant origins and resources..."
J.M. Roberts, History of the World

It is safe to say that more people believe in God than watch the Super Bowl, MTV, the World Series, the Olympics, the Indy 500, the Kentucky Derby, and the Oscars. More people believe in God than socialism, existentialism, and vegetarianism combined, and more people are invested in God than in the stock market. The difference is that people know what the words Super Bowl, MTV, socialism, and stock market mean. The word

God, however, is another story altogether, and has a wide range of beliefs throughout our planet.

The United States of America was founded on the principle of separation of church and state, and at the same time proclaims, *"Men are created equal, that they are endowed by their Creator with certain unalienable Rights..."* The Gallup Organization has found that 96% of Americans believe in God, and 90% pray regularly. Beyond the borders of America are another three and a half billion Christians and Moslems who worship the God that the Jews introduced to humankind.

Seeking to preserve their culture and start anew, Jewish immigrants departed familiar lands to pursue their own American dreams for more than 300 years. During some periods, Jews sought refuge in the United States from the horrors and tragedies of persecution, pogroms, and the Holocaust. During other times, they came to seek better lives and greater economic opportunities for themselves and their children. Jews became doctors where and when they were badly needed. When their professional path was limited, Jews became leaders of finance, and accumulated wealth (and power) as a result. Throughout history, Jews have been leaders in all areas of science, helping to advance human understanding of the world. The one thing that ties all Jews together is Judaism, and Judaism is rooted in Torah – its laws, stories, and ways of teaching values.

Torah is not just the Ten Commandments. It is not just the stories of our patriarchs (and matriarchs). It is not just the stories of our prophets. Torah is an intricate and detailed set of laws that govern human interaction and the development of human society. We are not successful merely in order to accumulate money, prizes, or self-serving power. We are not successful simply to perpetuate our people. We achieve greatness so we can be seen, so we can set an example to the world by how we live (I know it sounds egomaniacal, but just look at all we've contributed to mankind. Besides, it's also a great topic for one of those Saturday morning sermons).

From the very first Jewish immigrants to those arriving today in the 21st Century, the purpose for their immigration to America has been freedom and opportunity. In so many ways they faced a mighty struggle to gain the liberties they sought, and relied heavily on their own culture of discipline, study, and hard work to forge new opportunities for success and excellence. The United States would not be the country we know without the achievements of Jewish Americans. We have demonstrated that we can choose to maintain our cultural traditions while honoring the principles and beliefs that bind us together.

SAY IT LOUD AND SAY IT PROUD!!!

ABOUT THIS IDEA OF BEING THE "CHOSEN PEOPLE."

God gave Moses (and some believe Mel Brooks) the Ten Commandments on Mount Sinai to serve as principles of moral behavior for the human race. The Ten Commandments of God are the foundation of the moral code and legal system of justice for Western civilization. The architecture of the U. S. Supreme Court building reflects this biblical foundation. At the center of the sculpture over the east portico of the Supreme Court Building, there is the image of Moses holding the two tablets of the Ten Commandments; these are also engraved over the chair of the Chief Justice and on the bronze doors of the Supreme Court.

Nine year old Joseph was asked by his mother what he had learned in Hebrew school.

"Well, Mom, our teacher told us how God sent Moses behind enemy lines on a rescue mission to lead the Israelites out of Egypt. When he got to the Red Sea, he had his engineers build a pontoon bridge and all the people walked across safely. Then he used his walkie-talkie to radio headquarters for reinforcements. They sent bombers to blow up the bridge and all the Israelites were saved."

"Now, Joey, is that really what your teacher taught you?" His mother asked.

"Well, no, Mom. But if I told it the way the teacher did, you'd never believe it!"

There are few concepts in religion that are more emotionally loaded and more misunderstood than the belief that we are "the Chosen People." For some, if you are Jewish, the idea of "Chosen People" probably feels very uncomfortable — perhaps as an offensive, divisive, or outdated claim of superiority. Others may feel proud, pointing to the extraordinary achievement of Jews, and the very fact that we have miraculously survived for thousands of years in spite of constant persecution and attempts at annihilation. And if you are not Jewish this statement may sound like a claim that somehow God loves Jews better than others and has given them special treatment.

The Jewish concept of being the "Chosen People" is not a badge of superiority and separation. Quite the contrary. It is a humble call to action and responsibility. Jews specifically have been chosen to, or have chosen to, be of service to others so that the world may be a more just place. This is not a contrived creation, but rather a theological and historical fact.

It all began with Abraham, whose relationship with God has traditionally been interpreted in two ways: either God chose Abraham to spread the concept of monotheism, or Abraham chose God from all the deities that were worshiped in his time. Either way, the idea of "chosenness" meant that Abraham and his descendants were responsible for sharing the word of God with others. Though a nation with a massive standing army may have been the more logical choice to spread the word of God, the success of such a mighty people would have been attributed to their strength, not the power of God. But Abraham, according to the Bible, was the first human being to recognize the truth that everything and everyone emanates from the same Source. Whatever you believe about Abraham, that he was a real person, the mythologizing of a tribal chief, or a fabricated character, does not matter, because the reality is that Judaism has understood his story as a call to kindness and hospitality. God does not play favorites among His people, however, the Bible does tell us that God's chosen people are the Jewish race because they were the only ones to obey Him in lieu of other gods.

"Chosenness" continued when the Jews received the Ten Commandments at Mt. Sinai. Again, whether historical fact or fiction matters not one bit, because we do have the Ten Commandments, and they came to the world through the Jewish people.

Christianity and Islam account for more than half our planet's population (7.5 billion), believing monotheistically. 96% of Americans believe in a higher power. 85% believe in heaven. 82% believe in miracles, including 6% of them being atheists.

Now the big question. Is God male or female? Almost 40% of adults think God is male, while less than 1% believe God is female. That leaves many people believing God is neither male nor female. Surprisingly perhaps, more women (a lot more women) believe God is male, than do men. Although God is referred to in the Hebrew Bible with masculine imagery and grammatical forms, Jewish philosophy does not attribute to God either sex or gender. However, the single greatest statistic in all of this is that there is only one God. So I guess Abraham (and his descendants) did okay getting the word out.

SH'MA YISRAEL ADONAI ELOHEINU ADONAI EḤAD —

"HEAR, O ISRAEL: THE LORD IS OUR GOD, THE LORD IS ONE."

A.S. Winston

IMITATION IS THE SINCEREST FORM OF FLATTERY

In thinking of the golden civilizations and high points in history, the average Jew will conjure up images of pontificating Greek philosophers, Roman legions shimmering in the golden sun, and the artistic wonders of the Renaissance masters. Tell him that in terms of world history the Jews have outshone all these civilizations, and he will look at you in disbelief. He knows all about the Jews. They were the ones defeated by the Romans, slaughtered by the crusaders, expelled by the Spaniards, disemboweled by the Cossacks, and cremated by the Nazis. Every Jewish child studies in school about how each nation lived…and how the Jews died.

We gave the world the one true God. Today the name is Elohim, Jesus and Allah. The Hebrew bible's idea that all men are created as equals today goes by the name of democracy. The idea of a brotherhood of nations goes by the name United Nations. Consider also the teaching that one must love one's fellow man as oneself, is today called the Golden Rule.

The majority of the earliest settlers were, of course, Puritans. Beginning with the Mayflower, over the next twenty years, 16,000 Puritans migrated to the

Massachusetts Bay Colony, and many more settled in Connecticut and Rhode Island. Like their cousins back in England, these American Puritans strongly identified with both the historical traditions and customs of the ancient Hebrews of the Old Testament. They viewed their emigration from England as a virtual re-enactment of the Jewish exodus from Egypt. To them, England was Egypt, the king was Pharoah, the Atlantic Ocean was the Red Sea, America was the land of Israel, and the Indians were the ancient Canaanites. They were the new Israelites, entering into a new covenant with God in a new Promised Land. Thanksgiving, first celebrated in 1621, a year after the Mayflower landed, was initially conceived as a day parallel to the Jewish Day of Atonement, Yom Kippur; it was to be a day of fasting, introspection and prayer.

"The story of the Jewish people in America is a story of America itself. The pilgrims considered this nation a new Israel, a refuge from persecution in Europe. When the first Jewish settlers came to our shores, they were not immediately welcomed. Yet, from the onset, the Jews who arrived here demonstrated a deep commitment to their new land. Jewish Americans have made countless contributions to our land."
George W. Bush, President of the United States

A.S. Winston

A TESTAMENT OF HOPE

In 1909, when four Jews were among the sixty multiracial signers of the Call to National Action resulting in creation of the NAACP, the Yiddush newspapers on New York's Lower East Side were already equating the lynchings of African Americans in the South with pogroms against Jews in Russia. During the next half century, bonds and political cooperation between African American and American Jewish communities gradually matured. The culmination, in 1964, was Mississippi Freedom Summer, when over half the white students who journeyed south to fight for black voting rights were estimated to have been Jewish. Those drawn to the civil rights movement had a sense of selfless idealism, not only for the black community, but also in uprooting prejudices that victimized the Jewish community as well.

"How could there be anti-Semitism among Negroes when our Jewish friends have demonstrated their commitment to the principle of tolerance and brotherhood not only in the form of sizable contributions, but in many other tangible ways, and often at great sacrifice. Can we ever express our appreciation to the rabbis who chose to give moral witness with us in St. Augustine during our recent protest against segregation in that unhappy city?

Need I remind anyone of the awful beating suffered by Rabbi Arthur Lelyveld of Cleveland when he joined the civil rights workers there in Hattiesburg, Mississippi? And who can forget the sacrifice of two Jewish lives, Andrew Goodman and Michael Schwerner, in the swamps of Mississippi? It would be impossible to record the contribution that the Jewish people have made toward the Negro's struggle for freedom – it has been so great."

Martin Luther King, Jr., from a 1965 interview, in A Testament of Hope

Jews identified themselves forth-rightly with the Civil Rights movement of the 50's and 60s. In 1954, the United States Supreme Court rendered its judgment in Brown v. Board of Education, striking down racial segregation in public schools. Within the next dozen years, a series of federal laws and court orders shattered every legal support of racial segregation.

As far back as the 19th century, Jewish storekeepers were virtually the only Southern merchants who addressed black customers as 'Mr.' and 'Mrs.' and permitted them to try on clothing. By the early 20th century, a few Southern Jews even ventured to speak out against the evils of white supremacy. In 1929, Louis Isaac Jaffe, editorial writer for the Norfolk Virginia-Pilot, won the Pulitzer Prize for his denunciation of lynchings, not only in his home state, but throughout the South.

Julius Rosenwald, chairman of Sears Roebuck, contributed more generously in behalf of Southern blacks than did any philanthropist in American history. His benevolence was continued by his daughter, Edith Stern of New Orleans, whose Stern Family Fund in later years contributed vast sums to civil rights activities in the

South. It was known, too, that Southern Jews privately provided manpower and funds for civil rights causes.

Rabbi Julian Feibelman of New Orleans opened the doors of his Temple Sinai in 1949 for a lecture by Ralph Bunche, the black United Nations ambassador, permitting the first major integrated audience in New Orleans history.

At the height of the anti-integration effort, in 1957, Rabbi Ira Sanders of Little Rock, testified before the Arkansas Senate against pending segregationist bills. Rabbi Perry Nussbaum of Jackson, Mississippi, also courageously lent his support to the integration effort, as did Rabbis Jacob Rothschild of Atlanta, Emmet Frank of Alexandria, and Charles Mantingand of Birmingham.

If Southern Jews believed that a low profile would permit them to continue living peacefully, they were wrong. Klan groups exploited the integration crisis to launch acts of anti-Semitic violence. In one year, from November 1957 through October 1958, temples and other Jewish communal edifices were bombed in Atlanta, Nashville, Jacksonville, and Miami, and undetonated dynamite was found under synagogues in Birmingham, Charlotte, and Gastonia, North Carolina. Telephoned death threats to rabbis became routine.

Jewish participation in the Civil Rights movement far transcended institutional associations. One black leader in Mississippi estimated that, in the 1960s, the critical decade of the voter-registration drives, "as many as 90% of the civil rights lawyers in Mississippi were Jewish."

Jews similarly made up at least 30% of the white volunteers who rode freedom buses to the South, registered blacks, and picketed segregated establishments.

In their midst were several dozen Reform rabbis who marched among the demonstrators in Selma and Birmingham. A number of them were arrested.

Two young New Yorkers, Michael Schwerner and Andrew Goodman, served in 1964 as voting-registration volunteers in Meridian, Mississippi. One of their coworkers was a young black Mississippian, James Chaney. Together they were waylaid and murdered by Klansmen, their bodies dumped in a secret grave. As much as any single factor, it was the nationwide attention given the discovery of their corpses that accelerated passage of the Voting Rights Act of 1965. The Jews had long since achieved their own political and economic breakthrough. Rarely had any community gone to such lengths to share its painfully achieved status with others.

SAY IT LOUD, AND SAY IT PROUD!

"EDUCATION IS NOT THE FILLING OF A BUCKET, BUT THE LIGHTING OF A FIRE."

We all know how important education is to our souls. It starts with our very first breath. Known as "the people of the book," Jews valued education long before migrating to the United States. In America, education was (and still is) "the great leveler." It is the one thing that Jewish Americans embrace as a path to opportunity for themselves and their children.

Although settled "American Jews" created educational institutions to transform immigrants, clashing with the newcomers over their desire to preserve old world ways, it did not take long for East European Jewish immigrants to accept the public schools for the education of their sons and daughters. Despite the reverence for tradition on the part of new immigrant families, most parents wanted their children to learn the language and values of their new home.

Once upon a time there was not a single Jewish president of a major university. Today there are Jewish presidents at dozens of major institutions, including Dartmouth, Tufts, M.I.T., Harvard, Yale, Princeton, Cornell, Penn, Northwestern, U.C. Berkley, Stanford, McGill (Canada), CalTech, Carnegie Mellon, Adelphi, CCNY, Vermont, WestChester, Bard, Connecticut

College, Univ. of Denver, Nebraska, Swarthmore, Hartford, Brandeis, George Washington, Univ. of Chicago, Lafayette, Temple, Bradley, Babson, U.C. San Diego, Barnard, and Rice (to name just a few).

"Education is the passport to the future, for tomorrow belongs to those who prepare for it today."
--Malcomb X

It has been said that Israel's only true natural resource, apart from Dead Sea minerals, is the ingenuity of its people. Due to its emphasis on Torah study, Judaism is characterized by "lifelong learning" that extends to adults as much as it does to children. The tradition of Jewish education goes back to biblical times. One of the basic duties of Jewish parents is to provide for the education of their children. The importance of education is stressed in the Talmud. It is the seed to success. The more people who are educated, the better our society will function.

Education is a core value in Jewish culture and in Israeli society at large, with many Israeli parents sacrificing their own personal comforts and financial resources to provide their children with the highest standards of education possible.

Supporting education is a way of ensuring that the rich legacy of Jewish life, learning, values, and traditions will be transmitted to a new generation. We are guided by the traditional Jewish values of "torah," (tradition, learning and deeds), "tikkun olam" (improving the condition of our world), "tzedakah" (philanthropy and acts of loving kindness), and "k'lal Yisrael" (Jewish peoplehood).

In the last few years, the leaders of Israel's educational system have come to realize that technological developments have created a gap between modern adult society and the school environment. Furthermore, if Israel's advanced technological level was to be maintained and enhanced in the future, scientific know-how, and familiarity with modern tools, must be introduced to children as early as possible.

One outcome has been the introduction of a revolutionary program to "technologically-saturate" the learning environment starting in kindergarten, with computers aimed at upgrading the teaching of mathematics, science and technology throughout the school system. In Israel, computers have become the fourth basic element of education, which, for generations, were exclusive to the proverbial "three 'r's" - reading, writing and 'rithmetic.

As everywhere, the advancement of basic scientific knowledge is the chief objective of researchers at Israel's universities. In addition to their scientific research activities, the universities continue to play an important role in the country's technological advancement.

Today, more than 310,000 students are enrolled in Israel's universities, with about 21% of all undergraduate students and 50% of all Ph.D. candidates specializing in the sciences or medicine. Another 13% of all undergraduate students and 8% of all graduate students specialize in engineering and architecture

Education strengthens Jewish identity. It is designed to provide future generations an understanding on how we survived millennia after millennia, to create a better future. There is great power in education. Today, Israeli scientists continue to contribute to the advancement of agriculture, computer sciences, electronics, genetics, medicine, optics, solar energy and various fields of engineering, with Tel Aviv as one of the ten most technologically influential cities in the world, and Israel as having one of the world's most technologically-literate populations.

Education has also made us famous. Our direct ancestors are the stars of the greatest work of literature ever conceived, the Bible, which is adored by more than three billion of the world's people. It tells how we came to be. The Bible is our family album.

"Education is the most powerful weapon which you can use to change the world."
— Nelson Mandela

REWIND

The polio virus inflamed nerves in the brain and spinal cord, causing paralysis of the muscles in the chest, leg and/or arms. Lacking a vaccine, the nation tried to halt the spread of this "plague" by closing public pools and parks. Parents ordered their children not to drink from public water fountains. Schools canceled graduations as a precaution. The March of Dimes raised money for a cure. Few people who saw them will ever forget the organization's poster children, adorable kids with braces and crutches who posed in fund-raising pictures. Such was the horror created by this disease, a parent fearing their child spending the rest of his (or her) life in an iron lung. Two Jewish doctors vanquished that disease and removed such fears forever.

America has been blessed with many waves of immigrants from all over the world who have made our nation the most successful in history. This success has drawn these "newcomers" with its promise of living free and making one's own way, and perhaps achieving and contributing great things.

The first Jews arrived in 1654 fleeing the Inquisition. They insisted on, and were granted, full citizenship. One hundred of their successors fought in the Revolutionary War, and one, Haym Solomon, helped secure vital financing for George Washington's Revolutionary Army (in his honor, the U.S. Postal Service issued a stamp hailing Salomon as a financial hero of the American Revolution).

Waves of succeeding immigrants helped build American industries and culture, and our way of life. In 1850 there were about 17,000 Jews living in America. By 1880, there were 270,000. Most of these Jews moved to the New York area, which at this time had a population of 180,000. It would soon grow to 1.8 million.

In New York City, the Jewish area was the Lower East Side of Manhattan. The ones who "made it" quickly moved to the Upper East Side. And these Jews did remarkably well in the New World. Some famous names of those who 'made it' were: Marcus Goldman, founder of Goldman, Sachs & Co; Henry, Emanuel and Meyer Lehman, founders of Lehman Brothers; Abraham Kuhn and Solomon Loeb, founders of the banking firm Kuhn, Loeb and Co; Jacob Schiff, Loeb's son-in-law, and a major American financier; and Joseph Seligman, who started out as a peddler and who became one of the most important bankers in America.

Jews built the majority of the great retailing institutions like Macy's, Nieman Marcus, and Bloomingdale's. Even today, more recent names such as Home Depot and Costco have their origination in Jewish roots.

Our garment industry, with names like Levi's, Ralph Lauren, Calvin Klein, Donna Karan and others, changed the United States from a country in which garments were made by hand, one at a time, into the world's leader in ready-to-wear and high fashion.

Our computers, with names like Dell, software from giants like Oracle, search engines like Google, and social media like Facebook, share the legacy, just as Intel and Qualcomm chips and technologies are inside so many of our computers and cell phones.

The three largest broadcasting networks – ABC, NBC, and CBS – were built from the efforts of two visionary Jewish entrepreneurs, David Sarnoff and William Paley. Sarnoff in particular saw the potential to convert "wireless," (then used for ship-to-shore communications), into a broadcast medium distributed via a "network."

The technology for making movies was invented by the genius of Thomas Edison (not Jewish), but it was Jewish entrepreneurs who saw the potential to create an industry, making feature-length films, distributing them internationally, and building and sustaining the studios. From that arose the vital role played by Jewish producers, directors, and actors, making the motion picture industry the leader in world entertainment.

So many of the most important U.S. newspapers and book publishers came from, or were largely shaped by Jews, notably, The New York Times, The Washington Post, The Wall Street Journal, Random House, and Simon & Schuster. And in winning more than fifty percent of the Pulitzer Prizes for non-fiction, we confirm the importance of Jews in news writing.

History shows that if we attend a symphony, one third of the time the conductor will be Jewish. And if we watch the annual ceremony for the Kennedy Center honorees, we will be celebrating the fact that the same is true for one-fourth of our most important performing artists.

In medicine, law, science, politics, and education, the leadership, innovation and hard work of Jews have benefited us all. And if we have been disproportionately represented among the members of the Forbes 400, and as CEOs of the Fortune 500, that achievement is outstripped by the fact that in philanthropy, particularly for secular causes such as education, medicine, and the arts, Jews sincerely believe in tzedakah, and that their good fortune is to be shared.

And when the underprivileged in America have needed help, Jews were there. Julius Rosenwald, who built Sears Roebuck, was responsible for the construction of more than 5,000 schools for African Americans throughout the South when he found conditions appalling.

There can be little doubt that Jews have for centuries been substantially over-represented in many fields of learning and accomplishment. One must wonder, how could such a tiny, numerically insignificant group of people produce so many of this planet's most accomplished, and most influential citizens?

Jews comprise an amazing number of history's most important figures, people who have had a profound impact on humanity: the Patriarch Abraham, whose life and teachings are considered sacred by Jews, Christians, and Muslims; Moses, the lawgiver to Jews and Christians; Jesus and his disciple, Paul, who founded and spread Christianity.

That Jews were attracted to America is a testament to its greatness and hospitality to all immigrants. That we have repaid our welcome and relative freedom from discrimination with great achievements and contributions is equally clear.

The huge premium Jews have placed on education, on rearing strong families, our push for innovation and entrepreneurship, tolerance for differing opinions, accountability for one's performance in this life, and our sense of duty to help make the world better, is but a tiny sample of the cultural values that we have added to America's melting pot.

The Jews of this country have been ready to offer up life and fortune for America. We have been patriots in time of war, and philanthropists in time of peace. We will be patriots and philanthropists again in the future.

Jewish history is not a fairy tale, though sometimes it might seem like one. From the very first Jewish immigrants to those arriving today in the 21st Century, the purpose for our immigration to America (as I've noted over and over again), has been freedom and opportunity. Working on our own culture of discipline, education, and hard work, we've forged new opportunities for success and excellence. As a result of Jewish immigration, some of America's greatest cultural icons have emerged.

Consider a history of the movies without Samuel Goldwyn, or the Warner Brothers; American music without George and Ira Gershwin, Benny Goodman, and Leonard Bernstein; American song without Irving Berlin, Al Jolson, and Oscar Hammerstein II; American opera without Robert Merrill, Richard Tucker, or Beverly Sills; American magic without Harry Houdini; American jurisprudence without Louis Brandeis and Felix Frankfurter; American theater without Arthur Miller, Lillian Hellman, and Neil Simon; American baseball without Hank Greenberg and Sandy Koufax; American fashion without Ralph Lauren, Calvin Klein, and Donna Karan.

Imagine also the course of American physics without Albert Einstein, Robert Oppenheimer, or Leo Szilard. Imagine American medicine without Jonas Salk and Albert Sabin. Imagine the world of finance without Haym Salomon, Henry Morgenthau, and Bernard Baruch. Imagine American business without Michael Bloomberg, Levi Straus and Helena Rubenstein.

In every case, Jewish Americans have altered the course of their respective disciplines. Clearly, the families and descendants of Jewish immigrants to our shores have contributed mightily to virtually every aspect of the American landscape.

The American-Jewish community with their moral passion, intellectual energies and abilities, and financial clout, has attained success and acceptance beyond their forebear's fondest dreams. Though only a small minority within the United States, American Jews are influential far beyond their small percentage of the population. What we've accomplished is awesome.

We shouldn't have to apologize for our success. We share our success. We shouldn't have to apologize for our fortunes. We share our fortunes. We share our discoveries, through medicine, science, chemistry, economics, literature, and the arts. We brought the world the Ten Commandments. We introduced the world to one God. We gave the world the Bible and even their "Savior."

Maybe it is just an ongoing, never ending fairy tale. Or maybe, it's all about those two pennies. Regardless of the rationale you choose, why the hell shouldn't we be proud? Why shouldn't we acknowledge our success? Why shouldn't we say to the world, "I'M JEWISH AND I'M

PROUD," without fearing repercussions and anti-semitic backlash? Why shouldn't we kvell like everybody else does with their achievements?

"Death comes to all, but great achievements build a monument which shall endure until the sun grows cold." Ralph Waldo Emerson

SAY IT LOUD, AND SAY IT PROUD!

THE VOICES OF A PEOPLE...

"God, I know we are your chosen people, but couldn't you choose somebody else for a change?"
--Shalom Aleichem

"Pessimism is a luxury a Jew can never allow himself."
--Golda Meir

"What one Christian does is his own responsibility, what one Jew does is thrown back at all Jews."
--Anne Frank

"Hebrew, n. A male Jew, as distinguished from the Shebrew, an altogether superior creation."
--Andrew Bierce

"Even if you are Catholic, if you live in New York you're Jewish. If you live in Butte, Montana, you are going to be goyish even if you are Jewish."
--Lenny Bruce

"Anytime a person goes into a delicatessen and orders a pastrami on white bread, somewhere a Jew dies."
--Milton Berle

"I'm Jewish. I don't work out. If God had wanted us to bend over, He would have put diamonds on the floor."
--Joan Rivers

"In Jewish history there are no coincidences."
--Elie Wiesel

"I don't know why people get upset when you say there are a lot of Jewish people in the movie industry. That's the truth. That's like saying there are blacks in the NBA. That's not making a judgement, that's just a fact."
--Spike Lee

"The observant Jew has his own sense of values. Torah Judaism is his blueprint for this life, his target for existence."
--Meir Kahane

"There are two ways to live. You can live as if nothing is a miracle. You can live as if everything is a miracle."
--Albert Einstein

"To be a Jew is a destiny."
--Vicky Baum

"My father never lived to see his dream come true of an all-Yiddish-speaking Canada."
--David Steinberg

"Israel has created a new image of the Jew in the world - the image of a working and an intellectual people, of a people that can fight with heroism."
--David Ben-Gurion

"Look at Jewish history. Unrelieved lamenting would be intolerable. So, for every ten Jews beating their breasts, God designated one to be crazy and amuse the breast-beaters. By the time I was five I knew I was that one."
--Mel Brooks

"Passover affirms the great truth that liberty is the inalienable right of every human being."
--Morris Joseph

"Historically the profoundest meaning of Passover is something which sets Judaism apart from other religions. It marks the birth of a nation. Out of a mass of slaves, Moses fashioned a nation and gave them a faith."
--Philip S. Bernstein

"Every year during their High Holy Days, the Jewish community reminds us all of our need for repentance and forgiveness."
--Billy Graham

"America, rather, the United States, seems to me to be the Jew among the nations. It is resourceful, adaptable, maligned, envied, feared, imposed upon. It is warm-hearted, over-friendly; quick-witted, lavish, colorful; its people are travelers and wanderers by nature, moving, shifting, restless.
--Edna Ferber

"I'm going to marry a Jewish woman because I like the idea of getting up Sunday morning and going to the deli."
--Michael J. Fox

"Jerusalem is Israel's capital, will never be divided, and will remain the capital of the State of Israel, the capital of the Jewish people, for ever and ever."
--Benjamin Netanyahu

"People ask, how can a Jewish kid from the Bronx do preppy clothes? Does it have to do with class and money? It has to do with dreams."
--Ralph Lauren

"No one has the right to put the Jewish people and the State of Israel on trial."
--Ariel Sharon

"If you were there and the Romans or the Babylonians were about to destroy Jerusalem and you had the power to do something about it, would you sit and mourn and cry? Or would you turn the world upside down to change history? So what is stopping you? Overturn the world today!"
-- Rabbi Menachem Mendel Schneerson

"To be Jewish is to be specifically identified with a history. And if you're not aware of that when you're a child, the whole tradition is lost."
--Joyce Carol Oates

"I don't want to achieve immortality through my work. I want to achieve immortality through not dying."
--Woody Allen

"There are two things that are infinite, the universe and man's stupidity..... And I am not sure about the universe."
--Albert Einstein

"Let me tell you the one thing I have against Moses. He took us 40 years into the desert in order to bring us to the one place in the Middle East that has no oil!"
--Golda Meir

"Israel has its attractions. It's the most dramatic country in the world. Everybody's engaged. Everybody argues. When I leave Israel, I get a little bored."
--Shimon Peres

"Most Texans think Hanukkah is some sort of duck call."
--Richard Lewis

"It's a heritage to be proud of. And then, too, it's something that you can't escape because the world won't let you; so it's a good thing you can be proud of it."
—Ruth Bader Ginsburg, United States Supreme Ct. Justice

"Jewish introspection and Jewish humor is a way of surviving . . . if you're not handsome and you're not athletic and you're not rich, there's still one last hope with girls, which is being funny."
—Mike Nichols

"The miracle is this: the more we share the more we have."
--Leonard Nimoy

"I felt not only this enormous pride at being a Jew; I felt this enormous void at not being a better Jew."
—Ronald O. Perelman

"Freedom is the oxygen of the soul."
--Moshe Dayan

"It specifically says in the Torah that you can eat shrimp and bacon in a Chinese restaurant."
—Jason Alexander

"I will always stand with Israel. I can't tolerate people who criticize Israel without walking in their shoes. I hate the lies they spread and their lack of knowledge. I'm proud to stand up for the Israelis."
--Adam Sandler

"Yom Kippur is something I do alone, with nobody else, because I believe that my relationship with God is mine and mine only."
—Diane von Furstenberg

"Being a Jew is like walking in the wind or swimming: you are touched at all points and conscious everywhere."
--Lionel Trilling

"God must have been on leave during the Holocaust."
--Simon Wiesenthal

"How I wish we lived in a time when laws were not necessary to safeguard us from discrimination."
--Barbra Streisand

"The lion and the calf shall lie down together but the calf won't get much sleep."
  --Woody Allen

"You punch me, I punch back. I do not believe it's good for one's self-respect to be a punching bag."
  --Ed Koch, Mayor of New York City

"The view of Jerusalem is the history of the world; it is more, it is the history of earth and of heaven."
  --Benjamin Disraeli

"The Jews are the living embodiment of the minority, the constant reminder of what duties societies owe their minorities, whoever they might be."
  --Abba Eban

"You can tell the strength of a nation by the women behind its men."
  --Benjamin Disraeli

"If we ever hope to rid the world of the political AIDS of our time, terrorism, the rule must be clear: One does not deal with terrorists; one does not bargain with terrorists; one kills terrorists."
  --Meir Kahane

"A Jewish woman had two chickens. One got sick, so the woman made chicken soup out of the other one to help the sick one get well."
  --Henny Youngman

"Look at how a single candle can both defy and define the darkness."
--Anne Frank

"The world is a dangerous place to live; not because of the people who are evil, but because of the people who don't do anything about it."
--Albert Einstein

"A Bar Mitzvah is the time in his life when a Jewish boy realizes he has a better chance of owning a team than playing for one."
--Jerry Reinsdorf

"The security of Israel is a moral imperative for all free peoples."
--Henry A. Kissinger, Secretary of State

"Until we are all free, we are none of us free."
--Emma Lazarus

"My parents didn't want to move to Florida, but they turned sixty and that's the law."
--Jerry Seinfeld

"Let us recognize that we Jews are a distinct nationality of which every Jew, whatever his country, his station, or shade of belief, is necessarily a member."
--Louis Brandeis, U.S. Supreme Ct. Justice

"We've come from the same history - 2000 years of persecution - we've just expressed our sufferings differently. Blacks developed the blues. Jews complained, we just never thought of putting it to music."
— Jon Stewart

"A summary of every Jewish holiday: They tried to kill us, we won, let's eat!"
--Alan King

"The German debt to the Jewish people can never end, not in this generation and not in any other."
--Menachem Begin

"I remind everybody that the Sabbath was the Jewish gift to civilization."
--Edgar Bronfman, Sr.

"I feel the greatest reward for doing is the opportunity to do more."
--Jonas Salk

"I'd like to do a Jewish porno movie. I'd call it 'I DON'T WANT TO DO THAT."
--Jeff Ross

"My grandmother was a Jewish juggler: she used to worry about six things at once."
--Richard Lewis

"I think that everything I do tends to root for the underdog."
--Judd Apatow

"Jerusalem is the city where Jewish kings are buried and not Arab terrorists."
  --Yosef Lapid

"Above all, this country is our own. Nobody has to get up in the morning and worry what his neighbors think of him. Being a Jew is no problem here."
  --Golda Meir

"I was lucky to live in the 20th century, when gefilte fish could be purchased in a jar."
  — Barbara Cooper

"Only a life lived for others is a life worthwhile."
  --Albert Einstein

"On the whole, my family had always adopted a reserved attitude toward Zionism. But the devastation caused by the war and the extermination of six million Jews radically changed all of our former attitudes. The idea of a Jewish homeland acquired an intense emotional appeal; I myself became an ardent Zionist".
  --Baron Guy de Rothschild

"For evil to flourish, it only requires good men to do nothing."
  --Simon Wiesenthal

"The American Jewish story starts with Ellis Island, and the candy store in the Bronx."
  --Arthur Hertzberg

"I am proud to nominate the first Jewish candidate for vice president, my colleague and my friend Joseph Lieberman. Al Gore, you could not have made a better choice for the vice presidential candidate of the United States."
--Christopher Dodd, United States Senator

"I'm comfortable being old... being black... being Jewish."
--Billy Crystal

"The purity of Jewish upbringing - the restrictions that one carries through life being a 'nice Jewish girl' - what a burden."
--Lauren Bacall

"I know that following the Super Bowl, the winning quarterback generally announces that he is now 'going to Disneyland.' Well, ladies and gentlemen, this winning quarterback is going to synagogue -- Shabbat is coming!"
--Benjamin Brafman, after successfully defending Sean "Diddy" Combs

"I went to school without Jewish friends and did not have Jewish community centers to go to. So I was kind of like an odd duck, so to speak. There was a lot of anti-Semitism – I learned something from all of this and it wasn't to turn the other cheek."
--Stephen Spielberg

"Introductions are tricky in a lesbian relationship. It's a word game. To my friends she's my lover, to strangers and family members in denial she's my roommate, to Jehovah's Witnesses at the door she's my lesbian sex slave, and to my mother she's Jewish and that's all that matters."
--Denise McCanles

"After the holocaust in Russia you were not allowed to be religious. So my parents raised me Jewish as much as they could and came to America. I love my religion. I think it`s a beautiful religion."
--Mila Kunis

"I`m Jewish and this was the first time I experienced real anti-Semitism. Paris was scary...there were synagogues bombed and there was anti-Semitic graffiti all over the place. I was very angry. This is something I am passionate about."
--Kate Hudson

"Being Jewish and having lost relatives in the Holocaust, I've always been aware of the meaning of prejudice. These are things that have remained with me throughout my political career."
-    Senator Bernie Sanders

"There is something very, very, special, universal and easily identifiable among all Jews; it is beyond territory, it is something we all have in common."
--Ted Koppel

"Jews don't care about ancient rivalries. We worry about the humidity in Miami."
--Evan Sayet

"Ours is a country built more on people than on territory. The Jews will come from everywhere: from France, from Russia, from America, from Yemen... their faith is their passport".
--David Ben-Gurion

"I think Jews are the smartest people in the world."
--Rob Reiner

"I hate housework! You make the beds, you do the dishes and six months later you have to start all over again."
--Joan Rivers

"I never mind my wife having the last word. In fact, I'm delighted when she gets to it."
--Walter Matthau

"I don't think anyone has been slandered more than the Jews."
--Fidel Castro

"The Bible is the great family chronicle of the Jews."
--Heinrich Heine

"The Jews' greatest contribution to history is dissatisfaction! We're a nation born to be discontented. Whatever exists we believe can be changed for the better."
--Shimon Peres

"Montreal is a very cosmopolitan, sophisticated, erudite, educated, glorious city today. But it wasn't quite that way when I was growing up there. There was a lot of anti-Semitism. And I had to deal with that in an area of the city that had very few Jews."
--William Shatner

"Freedom begins with what we teach our children. That is why Jews became a people whose passion is education, whose heroes are teachers and whose citadels are schools."
--Jonathan Sacks

"The Ten Commandments are the most visible symbol because these commandments are recognized by Christians and Jews alike as being the foundation of our system of public morality."
--Pat Robertson

"I often hear them accuse Israel of Judaizing Jerusalem. That's like accusing America of Americanizing Washington, or the British of Anglicizing London. You know why we're called 'Jews'? Because we come from Judea."
--Benjamin Netanyahu

"Life is about not knowing and making the best of it without knowing what's going to happen next."
--Gilda Radner

"As a child my family's menu consisted of two choices—take it or leave it."
--Buddy Hackett

"If a blizzard means you don't have to go to work, but also can't go out to do anything fun, it's basically a Jewish holiday."
--Adam Newman

"We Jews have a secret weapon in our struggle with the Arabs; we have no place to go."
--Golda Meir

"Other people have a nationality. The Irish and the Jews have a psychosis."
--Brendan Behan

"Whenever we came to New York on Sundays, we went to Chinatown. To us that was a very Jewish thing."
--Sarah Jessica Parker

"To be or not to be is not a question of compromise. Either you be or you don't be."
--Golda Meir

"The opposite of love is not hate, it's indifference. The opposite of art is not ugliness, it's indifference. The opposite of faith is not heresy, it's indifference. And the opposite of life is not death, it's indifference."
-- Elie Wiesel

When Mel Brooks told his Jewish mother he was marrying an Italian girl, she said: "Bring her over. I`ll be in the kitchen - with my head in the oven".
--Anne Bancroft

"Roses are reddish, Violets are bluish, If it weren't for Christmas, We'd all be Jewish."
Benny Hill

"My ancestors wandered lost in the wilderness for forty years because even in biblical times men would not stop to ask directions."
- Elayne Boosler

"No country in the history of the world has ever contributed more to humankind and accomplished more for its people in so brief a period of time as Israel has done since its relatively recent rebirth in 1948."
--Alan Dershowitz

"The United States and Israel have a unique relationship based on our mutual commitment to democracy, freedom, and peace. Therefore, just as our commitment to these principles must be steadfast, so must our support for Israel."
--Senator John Boehner, Speaker of the House

"I'm tenacious, and I also have a quality where if you tell me I can't do something, if I know I can't do it, I'm the first to raise my hand and say, 'I can't do that.' But there is a big Bronx, New York Jew in me that just says, 'Really? Really? You think I - yes, I can. I can do it. I can do it.'

- Ellen Barkin

"When a Jew visits Jerusalem for the first time, it is not the first time, it is a homecoming."

--Elie Wiesel

"I'm used to being in the minority. I'm a left-handed gay Jew. I've never felt, automatically, a member of any majority."

- Barney Frank, member U.S. House of Representatives

"I'm a spiritual person, I'm an American, I'm a Jew, and all of those things influence every breath I take, everywhere I go."

- Mandy Patinkin

"Our mother was a very religious and observant Jew, our father less so. She was kind of driving the religious education, so for us it was more a burden and an obligation when we were kids at that age."

- Joel Coen

"It's hard for a Jew of my generation, an American Jew, not to romanticize Israel."

-- - David Mamet

"I came into the world a Jew, and although I did not live my life entirely as a Jew, I think it is fitting that I should leave as a Jew. I don't want to turn my back on a great and noble heritage."
- Felix Frankfurter, United States Supreme Ct. Justice

"As a Jew, it is my historic responsibility to defend the Jewish people. I feel this responsibility for the survival of the Jewish people. We're not going to accept any decision by anybody else about security of the State of Israel. It is our role and only our role."
- Ariel Sharon

"Even though I grew up as a Sephardic Jew in Brooklyn where we ate Syrian food and went to temple, it was still America."
- Isaac Mizrahi

"I've always felt robbed of something by people not knowing I was a Jew."
- Piper Laurie

"The purpose of the Jewish state is to secure the Jewish future. That is why Israel must always have the ability to defend itself, against any threat."
--Benjamin Netanyahu

"The only thing chicken about Israel is their soup."
--Bob Hope

"In Israel, in order to be a realist you must believe in miracles."
--David Ben-Gurion

"When Jewish children are murdered, Arabs celebrate the deed. The death of an Arab child is no cause for celebration in Israel."
--Theodore Bikel

"In Israel, a land lacking in natural resources, we learned to appreciate our greatest national advantage...our minds. Through creativity and innovation, we transformed barren deserts into flourishing fields and pioneered new frontiers in science and technology."
--Shimon Peres

"From the day I started to think politically and to develop my own moral values, from my earliest youth, I have been an ardent defender of Israel."
--Steven Spielberg

"You know, I get much more Jewish in Israel because I like the way that religion is done there."
--Natalie Portman

"In Israel we tend to be carried away by our emotions."
--Ehud Olmert

"I believe that the people of Israel are the chosen people of God."
--Jerry Falwell

"Israel is a country that respects freedom - freedom of assembly, freedom of speech and freedom of worship."
--George Pataki, Governor of New York State

"I believe in Judaism, I was raised a Jew, I'm happy to be one - and proud to be one."
  --Michael Bloomberg, Mayor of NYC

"I went to college because that's what you do in my family; you get an education no matter what–no matter if you just starred in your own TV show for five years and would prefer to go sit on a beach in Hawaii."
  --Mayim Bialik

"People lived in the same apartments for years. You'd meet a group of kids in kindergarten, and you'd still be with them in high school. No one ever left the neighborhood."
  --Fran Drescher

"Koolaid is goyish. All Drake's Cakes are goyish. Pumpernickel is Jewish, and, as you know, white bread is very goyish. Instant potatoes – goyish. Black cherry soda's very Jewish. Macaroons are very Jewish – very Jewish cake. Fruit salad is Jewish. Lime Jell-O is goyish. Lime soda is very goyish. Trailer parks are so goyish that Jews won't go near them."
  –-Lenny Bruce

"The Jewish people, ever since David slew Goliath, have never considered youth as a barrier to leadership."
  - John F. Kennedy, President of the United States

"The Jewish man with parents still alive, is a fifteen-year-old boy and will remain a fifteen-year-old until they die."
  - Philip Roth

"Though I am not religious in the least, I am very proud to be Jewish."
- Daniel Radcliffe

"I was always a little unsteady in my self-belief. Then there was the Jewish thing. I love being Jewish, I have no problem with it at all. But it did become like a scar, with all these people saying you don't look it."
- Lauren Bacall

"I grew up in the classic American-Jewish suburbia, which has a whole different sense of what it means to be Jewish than anywhere else in the world."
- Natalie Portman

"Twenty five percent of Israeli citizens are not even Jewish. Anybody can become an Israeli citizen if you qualify. Religion is not a criterion for citizenship."
- Alan Dershowitz

"The Jewish part of me is superstitious."
- Gwyneth Paltrow

"It's not bragging if you can back it up."
-    Muhammed Ali

"I am one of the happiest people I know. And that's a weird place to have arrived at from being a depressed Jewish kid."
- Debra Winger

"I don't think I have accomplished what I still have to accomplish. There is one thing that I would like to do, and that's to bring security and peace to the Jewish people."
 - Ariel Sharon

"As a Jew I am aware of how important the existence of Israel is for the survival of us all. And because I am proud of being Jewish, I am worried by the growing anti-Semitism and anti-Zionism in the world."
 - Steven Spielberg

"My mother should have been Jewish. She could have taught a class on how to induce guilt."
 - Lorna Luft

"I envy my Jewish friends the ritual of saying kaddish - a ritual that seems perfectly conceived, with its built-in support group and its ceremonious designation of time each day devoted to remembering the lost person."
 - Meghan O'Rourke

"I guess everything having to do with your background has some influence on how you tell stories, but it's hard to parse how growing up in a Jewish community in Minnesota really affected it."
 - Joel Coen

"Everybody ought to have a lower East Side in their life."
 --Irving Berlin

"I go to temple a lot less than I would like because when I do, people still look at me as if they think it's a publicity stunt."
--Sammy Davis, Jr.

"I've got the Jewish guilt and the Irish shame and it's a hell of a job distinguishing which is which."
-- Kevin Kline

"I'd work to make it hip again to spend time in our fabled and fabulous land. But with a Puerto Rican father and a Jewish mother, I would probably be better suited as mayor of New York."
- Geraldo Rivera

"Coming from Canada, being a writer and Jewish as well, I have impeccable paranoia credentials."
- Mordecai Richler

"I'm studying Kabbalah, which is really the essence of Jewish spirituality."
- Sandra Bernhard

"Zionism demands a publicly recognized and legally secured homeland in Palestine for the Jewish people. This platform is unchangeable."
- Theodor Herzl

"The United States Jewish population has made many vital contributions in all areas of our society in such ways as helping to develop the cultural, scientific, political and economic life of our country."
- Jon Porter

"The evidence of a Jewish civilization going back more than two millennia is overwhelmingly borne out in the archaeology of the region. The heritage of the Jews in Palestine is documented."
 - Jack Schwartz

"Anti-Semitism is a noxious weed that should be cut out. It has no place in America."
 --William Howard Taft, President of the United States

"I've always been supportive of the right of Israel as a state, and I've always fought against anti-Semitism, even in my own community."
 --Harry Belafonte

"The Jewish nation is indeed, the heart of the world and there is no reason for the existence of empires, kings, rulers, masses, or systems aside from their reaction to the Jewish people."
 - Meir Kahane

"I get anxious. That lovely Jewish guilt that comes with ancestry."
 - Maya Rudolph

"Without a Jewish state, the iron truth of history is that the Jewish people sooner or later become even more vulnerable to the next wave of anti-Semitism."
 - Jack Schwartz

"Like other important immigrant communities, the Jewish experience in the United States represents the ideal of freedom and the promise and opportunity of America."
- Jan Schakowsky

"I had a bat mitzvah, was confirmed, went to Jewish summer camp, I go to temple for the High Holy Days. I think, like most people in their early 20s, I kind of strayed away from it. I think once I have a family I'll be back into it."
- Lizzy Caplan

"I would like Israel to be a Jewish state, and therefore not to annex over 2 million Palestinians who live in the West Bank and the Gaza Strip to Israel, which will make Israel a bi-national state."
- Yitzhak Rabin

"My parents came to the United States in the early years of this century as part of a wave of Russian Jewish immigrants seeking freedom and opportunity in the New World."
- Daniel Nathans

"Me, I look in the mirror and all I see is this Jewish kid from Queens."
- David Krumholtz

"Even a secret agent can't lie to a Jewish mother."
- Peter Malkin

"To the rest of us the supreme vindication of the scholar's view lies in their invincible allegiance to the Jewish heritage - a steadfastness that has been matched only by that of their rescuers."
- Henrietta Szold

"I'm Jewish, so I don't know much about Easter eggs."
- Simon Kinberg

"I'm very spiritual and I'm Jewish by faith. I'm not a practicing Jew, I'm more of a recreational Jew. I celebrate the holidays and I try to inform my kids about their heritage because I think we all at some point have to defend our heritage and if they get picked on I want them to know why."
- Peter Segal

"Volleyball is a Jewish sport. It's fun, and nobody can get hurt."
- Gail Parent

"The most remarkable thing about my mother is that for thirty years she served the family nothing but leftovers. The original meal has never been found."
- Calvin Trillin

"I come from Williamsburg, Brooklyn. These days Williamsburg is kind of a hip area, but when I grew up there, the taxi drivers wouldn't even go over the bridge, it was so dangerous."
--Barry Manilow

"You've got to be taught to hate and fear."
-- Oscar Hammerstein II

"Catholics believe life begins at conception. Atheists believe that life begins at birth. Jews believe that life begins when the children leave home and the dog dies."
Author Unknown

"I coughed a lot, I don't know. I smoked marijuana twice -- didn't quite work for me,"
--Vermont Senator Bernie Sanders

"Being a Jew, one learns to believe in the reality of cruelty and one learns to recognize indifference to human suffering as a fact."
Andrew Dworkin

"My wife is Jewish, and therefore, it's my children's birthright to be Jewish."
Michael J. Fox

"I come from French Cajun Jewish people."
Shia LaBeouf

"All chefs are like Jewish mothers. They want to feed you and feed you and impress you. It's an eagerness to please."
Padma Lakshmi

"You can take the babushka off the Jewish mother and dress her up in a pair of fancy jeans and Marc Jacobs sling-backs, but she's still going to expect a passel of grandkids."
Ayelet Waldman

"The Israeli military plays more than a critical role in defending the citizens of the Jewish state. It also plays an important social, scientific and psychological role in preparing its young citizens for the challenging task of being Israelis in a difficult world."
Alan Dershowitz

"I don't really know of the Jewish tradition of comedy, only the Jewish tradition of not keeping your mouth shut. Complaining about all that is hard, unfair or ridiculous in life-having strong feelings, and not being able to suppress them. That, to me, is Jewish."
Fred Melamed

"MY FATHER'S JEWISH. MY MOTHER'S JEWISH. I'M JEWISH."
These are the words uttered by the American journalist Daniel Pearl the moment before he was murdered by jihidas in 2002.

OUR VOICES WILL NEVER AGAIN BE SILENCED....
SAY IT LOUD, AND SAY IT PROUD!

"THE BLAME GAME..."

"If Algeria introduced a resolution declaring that the earth was flat and that Israel had flattened it, it would pass by a vote of 164 to 13 with 26 abstentions."
Abba Eban, Israeli Ambassador to the United States and to the United Nations.

A hundred years ago, a thousand years ago, the attitude toward Jews has not changed. Under the best of circumstances, we were tolerated. At worst, we were annihilated. Jews today have transcended all barriers of indifference and hatred. As a race that's been subjugated to massacres, faced persecutions, discrimination, and expulsions throughout the world in different times and generations, the Jewish people continue not only to exist, but to flourish with great success.

In the late 1800s, Theodor Herzl and Chaim Weizmann founded Zionism, a political movement dedicated to the creation of a Jewish state. They saw the state of Israel as a necessary refuge for Jewish victims of oppression, especially in Russia, where pogroms were decimating the Jewish population. The Holocaust brought the need for a Jewish homeland into sharp focus for both Jews and for the rest of the world. Those who tried to flee Nazi Germany were often turned back due to immigration limitations at the borders of every country, including the

United States, Britain and Palestine. Many who were sent back to Germany ended up in death camps where they were systematically murdered. The newly-founded United Nations developed a partition plan, dividing Palestine into Jewish and Arab portions trying to resolve the problem of control. "The plan" was ratified in November 1947, and when the mandate expired on May 14, 1948 (and British troops pulled out of Palestine), the Jews of Palestine promptly declared the creation of the State of Israel, which was recognized by several Western countries immediately. The surrounding Arab nations however, did not recognize the validity of Israel, immediately declaring war on the newly created nation. Miraculously, the new state of Israel won this year-long war, as well as every subsequent Arab-Israeli war. Israel quickly became an important ally, with its resources, its people, and its technology in all fields producing great beneficial consequences.

I don't know what it will take to get Arabs/Muslims to want peace. It's hard to deter those that believe God wants you dead. But Jews must respond forcefully to anti-Semitism wherever it raises its ugly head. Whether the world likes it or not is irrelevant to Jewish survival. I sincerely believe if the Arabs put down their weapons today, there would be no more violence, but if the Jews put down their weapons today, there would be no more Israel.

Human psychology testifies how we perceive success in terms of collective aspects. For example, the world thinks Indians make the best engineers and doctors, Germans make the best automobiles and heavy machinery, and Spaniards the best wine. Jews on the other hand, have surpassed all cliché barriers. The majority of non-fiction Pulitzer Prize winners are Jews, Nobel awardees are Jews. Drs. Jonas Salk and Albert Sabin vanquished the polio disease and removed our fears of this horror forever. When you think of the garment industry, you think of names like Levis, Ralph Lauren, Calvin Klein, and Donna Karan. In the universe of technology, Dell, Oracle, Google, and Facebook, have become an integral part of our everyday lives. For so many of us, our computers and cell phones have become lifelines, thanks to the chips and technologies of Qualcomm and Intel. David Sarnoff and William Paley helped give birth to the ABC, NBC, and CBS broadcasting networks. In medicine, law, science, politics and education, the leadership, innovation, and hard work of Jews have benefited us all. And if we have been successful as entrepreneurs, disproportionately represented among the members of the Forbes 400 and as CEOs of the Fortune 500, that achievement is outstripped by the fact that in philanthropy, where tzedakah rules, we are even more philanthropic than we are wealthy (yes, I know you've heard this before, but it worth repeating).

Still how can we deny the obvious? The harder we try, the deeper into the quicksand we seem to sink. Consequently, as long as we're going to be blamed for everything, we must also acknowledge the following is 'our fault' as well....

For introducing the world to one God, the Ten Commandments, and the Bible, blame the Jews. For discovering the vaccination for Hepatitus B, the treatment for syphilis, identifying the first cancer virus, and finding the cure for polio, blame the Jews. For the creation of genetic engineering, the discovery of virtual reality, inventing the laser, the first micro-processing chip, the creation of holographic imaging, and discovering color photography, blame the Jews. For inventing the kidney dialysis machine, the defibrillator, the cardiac pacemaker, and the first oral contraceptive pill, blame the Jews. For Levi jeans, the sewing machine, pioneering the ready-to-wear garment industry, and Helena Rubenstein, Estee' Lauder, and Charles Revson administering to our egos and creating worlds of prestige cosmetics, blame the Jews. For creating America's department stores (Macy's, A&S, Saks, Neiman-Marcus, Bloomingdale's etc.), blame the Jews. For discovering the law of thermodynamics bringing in the atomic era, and expediting the end of World War II saving thousands of lives, once again we know where to point the guilty finger. For Starbuck's coffee, Dunkin' Donuts, and Ben & Jerry's, blame the Jews. For Hollywood, the motion picture industry, sound movies, and "Oscar," blame the Jews. For great newspapers (the New York Times, Washington Post, and Wall Street Journal), great magazines (Time, Newsweek, and U.S. News and World Report), a world of highly prized print media, and the Pulitzer Prize, blame the Jews. For the music of Irving Berlin, George Gershwin, and Bob Dylan, blame the Jews. For Shell Oil, Amoco Oil, and advances in the petroleum industry, blame the Jews. For the Guggenheim Museums and Smithsonian's Hirschorn Museum and Sculpture Gardens, blame the Jews. For discovering insulin, discovering that aspirin dealt with pain, discovering chloral hydrate for convulsions, discovering streptomycin, and for discovering the origin and spread of infectious diseases, once again, blame the Jews. For being at the forefront of stem-cell research, which will, in the near future, give humanity unprecedented medical treatment for degenerative diseases, blame the Jews. For Superman, L'il Abner, Popeye, Batman, Spiderman, and Bugs Bunny, blame the Jews. For giving birth to the Broadway musical, blame the Jews. For creating the fashion industry, blame the Jews. For a world of laughter, blame the Three Stooges, the Marx Brothers, and a very long list of very funny Jewish comedians. For Las Vegas (there's no getting away from this one) blame the Jews. For being among the world's greatest philanthropists, donating billions and billions of dollars to education, medicine, science, the arts (and hundreds of additional charities), blame "tzedakah." For the conception of men and women as individuals with unique destinies, and the sense that tomorrow can be better than today, blame the Jews. For Sandy Koufax, Woody Allen, Mel Brooks, Albert Einstein, Jesus of Nazareth, Sigmund Freud, Barbra Streisand, Golda Meir, Stephen Spielberg, Isaac Asimov, Abraham, Al Jolson, John Steinbeck, Dr. Jonas Salk, Arthur Fiedler, Solomon R. Guggenheim, Yasha Heifetz, Boris Pasternak, Moses Montefiore, Zero Mostel, Albert Schweitzer, Hedy Lamarr, Leonard Bernstein, Benny Goodman, Baron Edmund Rothschild, Louis B. Mayer, Benjamin Disraeli, along with so many others (you saw the partial list in the introduction), blame their parents.

For the idea of the equality and dignity of each individual culminating in the declaration that "All men are created equal," and for the teaching that one must love one's fellow man as oneself, which today is called "the Golden Rule," most definitely blame the Jews.

Personally, I believe the Jews are the most wonderful and celebrated nation in the world! We are the descendants of some of the greatest people who ever walked the earth; from Abraham to King David and Albert Einstein…we have what to be proud of! And every Jew knows that God chose us to bring light unto the nations and subsequently wrote an entire book about it (the Torah). What could be more inspiring? Nothing should make a person prouder than being part of a people with a national mission to fix the world. We appreciate every moment of life. So stop, pause, and raise your glass to the delicious opportunity life is giving us right now. L'Chaim! And always remember, to SAY IT LOUD, AND SAY IT PROUD!

THE FUTURE IS ALWAYS BEGINNING TODAY

Everyone knows the story of the "little engine that could." By all rights, this engine was definitely not ready for the gargantuan task before him. He was not big enough. He was not built for that level of challenge. And yet, the little engine believed in himself, chanting "I think I can, I think I can," over and over, until he achieved his goal. A cute kids story, yes, but it's also a helpful reminder that no matter what obstacles you may encounter, keep believing in yourself and you will be able to conquer anything, with optimism, hard work, and perseverance.

And then there's David and Goliath. The tale of the underdog against the unstoppable foe, is one that resonates throughout history. In life you're bound to come across lots of challenges, sometimes big, sometimes enormous. But the size of the challenge is irrelevant. The only thing that determines what's possible for you is your mindset and your beliefs. Whether the hero is a person fighting a giant, or a newborn nation trying to emerge from a world of hostility that surrounds them, we always root for the underdog. There's something undeniably fulfilling about the 'weak' conquering the strong.

On May 14, 1948, in Tel Aviv, Jewish Agency Chairman David Ben-Gurion proclaimed the State of

Israel, establishing the first Jewish state in 2,000 years. In an afternoon ceremony at the Tel Aviv Art Museum, Ben-Gurion pronounced the words "We hereby proclaim the establishment of the Jewish state in Palestine, to be called Israel," prompting applause and tears from the crowd gathered at the museum. Ben-Gurion became Israel's first premier.

In the distance, the rumble of guns could be heard from fighting that broke out between Jews and Arabs immediately following the British army withdrawal earlier that day. Egypt launched an air assault against Israel that evening. Despite a blackout in Tel Aviv, and the expected Arab invasion, Jews joyously celebrated the birth of their new nation, especially after word was received that the United States had recognized the Jewish state. At midnight, the State of Israel officially came into being upon termination of the British mandate in Palestine.

The state that the United Nations "gave" Israel was 80% desert. We started it from zero. Today, we have a beautiful country, a powerful Army, a strong Air Force, and a thriving high tech industry. Intel, Microsoft, and IBM have all developed their businesses in Israel. We've turned the desert into a prosperous land. Our medical research continues to be groundbreaking and is among the finest in the world. Israeli scientists continue winning Nobel prizes in chemistry and economics. We've launched our own satellites into space. Israel today is among the few powerful nations that have nuclear technology and capabilities (no one will admit it, but everyone knows it).

Not too long ago, Jews were brought to death like sheep to slaughter. We crawled out from the burning crematoriums of Europe. Before the country took its first breath, Lebanon, Syria, Iraq, Jordan, Egypt, Libya, and Saudi Arabia, all attacked at once. We've won all our wars. With a little bit of nothing, and nowhere to go, a group of stubborn people built an empire. We overcame everything. We overcame the Greeks. We overcame the Romans. We overcame the Spanish Inquisition. We overcame the Russian pogroms. We overcame Hitler, Germany, and the Holocaust. And we overcame the armies of the Arab world. Today, the condition of the Jewish nation has never been better. The state of Israel is truly a fantastic success story, perhaps one of the greatest success stories of the 20th century, with an Israeli culture, a renewal of the Hebrew language, and a nationality among the world's happiest people.

Israel has built a thriving country that protects the rights of its citizens, protects freedom of religion and ensures that all religions have access to their religious sites. Israel protects a free press, minority rights and women's rights in a part of the world where such rights and protections are alien. By any yardstick you choose, educational opportunity, economic development, women and gay's rights, freedom of speech and assembly, legislative representation, Israel's minorities fare far better than any other country in the Middle East.

During the 20th century, when the vast majority of the 850,000 Jews who were living in Arab countries and Iran had to flee for their lives, leaving behind billions of dollars in property in their hundred, or even thousand-year-old communities, Israel provided a safe haven for approximately 600,000 of these Jewish refugees. Israel continues to provide a welcoming country for Jews who are fleeing the often violent anti-Semitism that they encounter today around the world.

Jews and Israel are living up to the requirement of "tikkun olam" - healing the world - as no other people and no other nation have done. Ample reason to let the world know why you are proud to be a Jew.

Today, Israel is home to a widely diverse population from many ethnic, religious, cultural and social backgrounds. Relative to the size of its population, Israel is the largest immigrant-absorbing nation on earth. Immigrants come in search of democracy, religious freedom, and economic opportunity.

Having an energetic can-do spirit, and a young society with ancient roots, Israel is home to over 8.4 million citizens, a mosaic of people living together and contributing to its vibrant democracy. Freedom of faith and worship is a cornerstone of Israeli democracy.

Never mind which country or culture tries to erase us from the world, we will continue to exist and persevere. Israel, the Bible nation, from slavery in Egypt, is still here, still speaking the same language. We are an eternal nation, and as long as we keep our identity, we will stay eternal.

Israel has surpassed the dreams of its founders. But time only flows in one direction, and without a pause button. Tomorrow looms on the horizon with a world of familiar and unforeseen challenges. The dreams of the future are always better than the history of the past. I don't know what life in the next century will be like, but of one thing I'm certain. Jewish women will be lighting

Shabbos candles. Such is the power of Jewish ritual, and it speaks to the eternity of the Jewish people.

SAY IT LOUD, AND SAY IT PROUD......*"I AM PROUD TO BE A JEW."*

Say It Loud, And Say It Proud

9 781981 637317